The Little Black Book of
MICROCAP INVESTING

Beat Wall Street with NASDAQ /AMEX Microcap Stocks, OTCBB Penny Stocks, and Pink Sheet Stocks

Dan Holtzclaw

Published by:
Greek Financial Services, LLC
P.O. Box 2595
Germantown, MD 20875-2595

Cover Design: Dale Schroeder, SDS Designs

First Edition August 2006
ISBN 0-9674758-2-1

CONTENTS

DEDICATION

To Trisha, Lauren, and Gillian.

ACKNOWLEDGEMENTS

The creation of this book would not have been possible without the hard work and dedication of many individuals. Having said as much, I would like to personally thank the following people who greatly contributed to this text:

Cromwell Coulson, Chairman and CEO of the Pink Sheets
Peter Toscano, CEO of International Power Group
Roy Warren, CEO of Bravo! Foods International Corp.

To the thousands of penny stock investors who spend their valuable time posting messages on the bulletin boards. I refer to their postings regularly for both research and relaxation. Although I have never met many of them in person, I have forged many valuable friendships with posters on the boards. These are the people who make penny stock investing interesting and enjoyable.

DISCLAIMER

Disclosure in terms of the Securities Act of 1933

In accordance with the provisions of section 17(b) of the Securities Act of 1933, which reads as follows (for the sake of completeness, section 17(b) is quoted in its entirety) it is hereby disclosed that: "Use of interstate commerce for purpose of offering for sale. It shall be unlawful for any person, by the use of any means or instruments of transportation or communication in interstate commerce or by the use of the mails, to publish, give publicity to, or circulate any notice, circular, advertisement, newspaper, article, letter, investment service, or communication which, though not purporting to offer a security for sale, describes such security for a consideration received or to be received, directly or indirectly, from an issuer, underwriter, or dealer, without fully disclosing the receipt, whether past or prospective, of such consideration and the amount thereof. "

The names of certain investors and message board posters have been changed to protect their identity. Any resemblance of these changes to actual persons is purely coincidental. Charts used in this book have been compiled from sources believed to be reliable. The author of this book cannot guarantee the accuracy and timeliness of the information contained in these charts. The author of this book will not be liable to anyone for any misinterpretation, inaccuracy, error, or omission of information in the charts. The author of this book is not associated with any NASD or NYSE firm. The author of this book is an independent investor and does not make any claim to be a stockbroker, securities analyst, certified financial planner, etc. As such, the context of this book is intended for informational and entertainment purposes only. By purchasing this text, you acknowledge that the author cannot be held responsible for the actions of individual investors and that all investments made by those who read this book are done so on their own merit. The author of this book is not responsible for any losses, monetary or otherwise, incurred by the readers of this book. At no time should any of the information in this book be considered as a solicitation or recommendation to buy, sell, or hold certain securities. While the information contained in this book has been compiled from sources believed to be reliable, the accuracy and truthfulness of this information cannot be guaranteed. All statements contained in this book are the opinion of the author and should not be construed as investment advice. Investors should fully investigate and understand the risks associated with investing before placing any money into the stock market. Investors should rely on sources of information other than this book prior to making investment decisions. Certain statements contained within this book constitute forward-looking statements within the meaning of Section 27A of the Securities Act of 1933 and 21E of the Exchange Act of 1934. Such statements include, without limitation, information regarding business and financing, business trends, future operating revenues and expenses. Forward looking statements are based on expectations, estimates, and projections that may change due to risks and uncertainties which could cause actual results or events to differ materially from those presently anticipated.

Any and all trademark rights apply to applicable companies, products, technologies, and/or any trademarked or copyrighted material referenced in this book. At no time should the inclusion of a company's name, products, technology, or services be construed as an endorsement of this book by said company or vice versa..

In general, the author tried to avoid mentioning stocks in which he holds positions. Additionally, the author of this book did not receive payment or any form of compensation for inclusion of companies in this book. Concerning specific stocks mentioned in this book, the author has the following relationship:

AFPC: No current position in stock or relationship to company
AMRE: No current position in stock or relationship to company
AMZN: No current position in stock or relationship to company
AQNT: No current position in stock or relationship to company
BLLI: No current position in stock or relationship to company
BMD: No current position in stock or relationship to company
BRVO: No current position in stock or relationship to company
CEP: No current position in stock or relationship to company
CFC: No current position in stock or relationship to company
CNES: No current position in stock or relationship to company
DRYS: No current position in stock or relationship to company
EGLE: No current position in stock or relationship to company
EVOL: No current position in stock or relationship to company
EVCI: No current position in stock or relationship to company
FFI: No current position in stock or relationship to company
FZN: No current position in stock or relationship to company
GLBT: No current position in stock or relationship to company
GSTL: No current position in stock or relationship to company
IPWG: The author frequently trades this stock and may hold positions of varying size depending on the date. At the time of publication of this book, the author has no compensatory relationship with this company.
JCOM: No current position in stock or relationship to company
JDSU: No current position in stock or relationship to company
LDIS: No current position in stock or relationship to company
LEND: No current position in stock or relationship to company
LVCP: No current position in stock or relationship to company

NETG: No current position in stock or relationship to company
NEW: No current position in stock or relationship to company
NT: No current position in stock or relationship to company
NXXI: No current position in stock or relationship to company
PLNI: No current position in stock or relationship to company
QBID: No current position in stock or relationship to company
QTCE: No current position in stock or relationship to company
RHWC: The author frequently trades this stock and may hold positions of varying size depending on the date. At the time of publication of this book, the author has no compensatory relationship with this company.
RNE: No current position in stock or relationship to company
SCHK: No current position in stock or relationship to company
SYD: No current position in stock or relationship to company
TASR: No current position in stock or relationship to company
TBSI: No current position in stock or relationship to company
TMY: No current position in stock or relationship to company
TSIG: No current position in stock or relationship to company
WZEN: No current position in stock or relationship to company
XKEM: No current position in stock or relationship to company

In many portions of this book, specific companies are mentioned while their stocks are not discussed. In all cases, please note that the author holds no position in the stocks of these companies nor does the author have a compensatory relationship with any of these companies.

PREFACE

Wow! Time sure does fly. It has been nearly seven years since I wrote *Penny Stocks: The Next American Gold Rush* and much has transpired during this time. Of course, concerning investors, the most important event during this timeframe was, without question, the bear market of 2000-2002. After enjoying unprecedented gains in the latter part of the millennium, the high flying bull markets came to a grinding halt and the face of investing was forever changed. This was a very unique time that may never be repeated again. The combination of business rushing to embrace the internet coupled with the general public's newfound access to online investing created optimum conditions for market appreciation. This was one of the fastest growing markets of all time and everyone wanted a piece of the action.

Remember those old e*Trade commercials with the kid telling his butler to mow the lawn? Or how about the one where the guy quits his job after seeing his stock jump and then quickly realizes his mistake when the stock tanks two seconds later? Ah, those were to the good ole days! There was an aura of giddiness in the air and it seemed as if *everyone* was making money. This was especially true in the penny stock community.

Prior to the internet explosion of the mid to late 1990's, penny stocks were often treated as the pariahs of the investing community and considered taboo by many. But as the online brokerages began to afford the average Joe the opportunity to invest his hard earned money, a curious thing happened. The allure of quick gains and unimaginable wealth attracted the common man to penny stocks in droves. Trading volume on the OTCBB exploded! Websites devoted to penny stock investing popped up like weeds following a drenching rain. Message boards were the hotbed of penny stock investors and generally resembled a busy bee hive teeming with active drones. The excitement was so palpable that you could literally sense it radiating from your computer screen. Some even went so far as to call this feeling "irrational exuberance" and warned of its impending doom.

We were told that our world was coming to an end, but did we want to listen? Heck NO! How could we hear this doom and gloom when there was a MOMO play on the way? There was money to be made and those who snoozed missed the boat. Well, we all know that our world did come to an end, at least temporarily. The market crashes beginning in March of 2000 followed by the tragedy of September 11, 2001 effectively killed the penny stock market as we knew it.

So, did penny stocks turn out to be the "Next American Gold Rush" as I so boldly stated in my previous work? Honestly, I would have to say yes. Much like the California Gold Rush of the 1800's, the beginning of the Penny Stock Gold Rush produced gains that were fast and furious. Just as the old 49er's could simply panhandle the river and come up with a plateful of riches, penny stock investors could almost blindly pick a stock and eventually come out with enormous gains. With such success, both eras attracted hordes of prospectors with dreams of finding the mother lode. A few investors found riches while others could only drum up despair. Did you know that of the millions of fortune seekers that trekked to California, only a very small percentage actually found the gold that they so desperately longed for? Following the market crash of the early millennium, penny stock investors found themselves in a parallel situation. Both phenomenons went from boom to bust in similar timeframes, producing winners, losers, euphoric success, and depressing heartbreak.

Why am I writing this book seven years after my first text you ask? Is the Penny Stock Gold Rush poised to make a return?

Can we once again look forward to the weekly MOMO play and chatrooms abuzz with exciting rumors and unabashed hype? Well, as they say in the car rental commercial, “Not exactly.” In the ensuing text, I will tell you why I think that now is the time to return to the pennies, pinks, and other microcaps in general. I will provide you with analysis of stocks that have successfully made the jump from the OTCBB to larger exchanges. I will describe sectors of the economy in which I am anticipating explosive future growth and the microcap companies that are poised to conquer them. You are in for an exciting and informative read!

1

FALL FROM GRACE

Time after time, people ask me when penny stocks will get "hot" again. Heaven knows that things definitely cooled off during the bear market of 2000-2002. One might even go so far as to say that, concerning penny stocks, the environment was downright frigid! In order to figure out the future of penny stocks, I think that it is prudent to first reflect upon their recent past. As they say, history tends to repeat itself and those that fail to learn from their mistakes are doomed to repeat them.

In the mid to late 1990's conditions were brewing for "the perfect storm" of investing. Strong economic conditions fueled enormous domestic growth and individual income was on the rise. A majority of American households owned a personal computer and many people were getting acquainted with a relatively "new" technology called the internet. Though the internet had been around in various forms since the late 1960's, it was not until the mid 1990's that mainstream America found it a useful and, eventually, an indispensable tool. The information superhighway was destined to be the renaissance of the twentieth century. Much like the way that advancements such as electricity and the automobile fundamentally changed our lives and culture, the internet would soon accomplish the same. Websites such as Amazon.com allowed consumers to shop from the comfort of their own home. Sites such as eBay.com allowed average ordinary people to peddle goods to the masses. No brick and mortar store required! Imagine that, you could make money without ever setting foot outside of your front door. Amazing! Unlike your local paper's classified section that allowed you to reach your immediate locale, the internet allowed you to reach the entire world! Search engine sites such as Yahoo.com, Excite.com, and Lycos.com put information at your fingertips. If you wanted to get data on a particular subject you simply typed in your query and a dozen links popped up to provide the answer. No more bound sets of encyclopedias were needed. Sadly, this led to the demise of the venerable door to door encyclopedia salesman, but who liked those guys anyway?

Yes, the internet was changing our lives for the better, but the best was yet to come. Just as America was beginning its online love affair, a number of financial firms began to offer investment services via the internet. Companies such as e*Trade, Ameritrade, Scottrade, and Web Street afforded the common man with an opportunity to partake in Wall Street's once seemingly untouchable riches. No longer would the stock market be the exclusive bastion of the rich and online brokerage firms went out of their way to ensure that this message reached the masses.

While it could easily cost you upwards of sixty dollars to make a trade with a live broker via the traditional route, an online trade could be executed for as little as five bucks. Hmm, five bucks or sixty, which to choose? Obviously, a majority of investors went with the cheaper option. While the online version of investing was much less expensive than that of the traditional brick and mortar brokerage firm, it was lacking in certain services. With an online firm, you did not have an advisor to provide you with investment advice. This fact scared many in the financial community as it was perceived that the common man did not possess the intellect to decipher the intricacies of the stock market. Hogwash I say! I don't know about you, but my personal experience with stock brokers has not been pleasant. At one time or another, I have utilized the services of brokers from many of the top firms in the country. In every case, the brokers wanted me to buy funds from companies that they "represented". Never did any of these brokers ever provide me with a hot tip or suggestion. If I wanted to do any trading, I had to do everything myself. I had to screen the stocks and find potential winners. I had to perform the due diligence. I had to determine entry and exit points. The only involvement my broker had in this process was charging me sixty smackers for pushing a button on his computer. This was ludicrous! Why was I giving this guy my hard earned money when I had to do all of the work? Needless to say, I gave my broker the boot and switched all of my accounts to online firms.

Like me, many investors also took advantage of online investment firms. The public's newfound access to online investing coupled with exuberant speculation concerning all things internet led to unprecedented market gains. This was especially evident in the tech heavy NASDAQ that was fully loaded with freshly minted internet stocks. In just a few years time the NASDAQ composite index rose from a paltry 1000 to a high of over 5000. No matter what you did, it *seemed* as if you could not lose.

This feeling of brazen confidence led many investors to the Over-the-Counter-Bulletin-Board (OTCBB) market. The OTCBB was home to the "penny stock" and was feared by many old school investors. More often than not, these investors were the same guys who relied on traditional brokers for investing advice. To be honest, their fears of penny stocks were well founded. In the late 1990's, I liken the OTCBB to the Wild West of the 1800's. Times were fast and furious, exciting, and lawless. In the course of a single day you could make a fortune or lose the shirt off of your back. There were MOMO plays, gappers, and pump & dumps. Fraudulent companies peppered the OTCBB landscape and various online stock promoters prowled the scene like bandits waiting for their next victim. In spite of these potential pitfalls, the allure of ten baggers was too great to dissuade investors and the OTCBB enjoyed a tremendous surge in trading activity. From 1993 to its peak in the year 2000, daily trading volume on the OTCBB increased by nearly 1100%!

Websites such as Ragingbull.com, Silicon Investor.com, and Bobz.com were part of the driving force behind the growth of the OTCBB market. The message boards on these sites proved to be hotbeds of activity with thousands of messages posted daily. For you see, unless they were writing an exposé about boiler room scams, large media press did not tend to cover the "insignificant" penny stock market. Without media coverage, where were investors supposed to find information on hot penny stocks? For all intensive purposes, the online message boards effectively served as the "Wall Street Journal" for OTCBB investors. To be perfectly honest, the penny stock message boards were more like a combination of the Wall Street Journal and the National Enquirer. Quite an odd combination, huh? For a typical one hundred posts, fifteen were usually spam advertising various websites or newsletters, twenty were people trading insults, another twenty were people pumping the stock with baseless claims, ten posts would be pumping other random stocks, thirty posts were relentless bashing, and if you were lucky, there might be five posts that actually contained some useful information. When a stock was hot, its message board could receive over one thousand posts per day! Many of the messages came from posters utilizing multiple aliases. When you surfed the bull boards long enough, you could easily pick out the paid bashers and pumpers. All you had to do was look at their posting style. Sometimes these professional posters would hold imaginary conversations with themselves through their various aliases! The boards were downright schizophrenic at times.

For the newbie investor that had migrated to the OTCBB from the more traditional exchanges, things could be quite confusing. The less regulated OTCBB and Pink Sheet markets were quite different from the NYSE and NASDAQ. Different regulations, different types of companies, and different trading policies confounded many investors. In this confusion, many people learned lessons the hard way…by losing money! That is why I decided to write my previous book. I grew tired of watching people make the same mistakes over and over. At the time, there had not been a book published on penny stock investing for nearly ten years. How were people supposed to learn the basics of penny stock investing? If they read any run of the mill investment text, it usually told them to avoid penny stocks like the plague! This simply would not do. With the ever increasing number of new penny stock investors, a basic text for entry level penny stock investing was sorely needed.

My last book was released in late 1999. At that time the markets were booming and times were good. Little did we know that within six months of its release, everything would soon change. Prior to the market collapse, Federal Reserve Board Chairman Alan Greenspan warned investors of "irrational exuberance" leading to unduly escalating stock prices. In fact, Greenspan first made this speech at the Annual Dinner and Francis Boyer Lecture of the American Enterprise Institute for Public Policy Research in December of 1996. Well, here it was three years later in 1999 and the markets showed no signs of slowing. Did Greenspan know what in the world he was talking about? While the markets kept rising higher and higher, naysayers began to speak a bit louder. You know those guys who say, 'Repent for the end is near!"? Well, that is what many stock analysts sounded like in the late 1990's. "How could an internet company that loses millions of dollars have a market cap greater than Ford or General Electric?" "When will the internet bubble burst?" Blah, blah, blah…these guys were moving their lips, but no one was listening. As long as the markets were moving north and people were making money, no one gave a darn what these analysts had to say. All of this would soon change in March of 2000.

The NASDAQ hit its high at just a shade over 5,000 on Friday March 10, 2000. Astonishing! In just a few short years, the NASDAQ had reached levels that took the DOW decades to achieve. Where was the crash? When was this so-called "internet bubble" going to bust? Soon…very soon! During the first three trading days of the ensuing week the NASDAQ fell nearly 10% to 4,582. Panic! Pandemonium! Was this it? If the market fell that fast in just three days, what would stop it from falling further? Temporary relief was found in the form of bargain hunters as they picked up shares of battered stocks and allowed the NASDAQ to quickly rebound to 4,963. Was that little dip the market correction that everyone was talking about? We could only wish! No, that little dip was just a taste of the pain that was soon to come.

By the beginning of April 2000, the NASDAQ had fallen 16% off of its highs, putting it well within the confines of a market correction. Was *this* the bursting of the internet bubble? Almost, but not quite. On April 14, 2000 all hell broke loose and the NASDAQ fell 355.49 points. By the end of the month, the market was nearly 34% off of its all-time high. It was quite depressing.

I remember one particular day that put things into perspective for me. The day was April 20, 2000. I was getting hammered in the market that day when a breaking news story hit the wires. A pair of deranged teenagers in Colorado had opened fire on their high school killing and wounding dozens of their fellow students. I remember thinking to myself that the thousands of dollars I had lost that trading day were insignificant compared to what was transpiring at that school. April 2000 was not a good month.

As the internet bubble began to burst, it was quite humbling to see the hubris of tech investors crushed in just a few short weeks. What happened to the invincible internet stocks? These were the pillars of the new "e" economy. How could they crumble so quickly? We were warned of this, but we did not want to listen. It's funny how easily our emotions turn. When times were good, we turned a deaf ear towards those who warned us of the reckless valuation of the NASDAQ. However, when the markets began to tank, we scurried like rats trying to escape a sinking ship. Analysts noted, "Investors are jumping out of anything that lacks justification for a solid valuation." Over the next eighteen months, the market sold off to a low in the 1,400's. From its high in March of 2000, the NASDAQ corrected over 70%! This precipitous drop in market valuation is second only to the market crashes of 1929-1932 that started the Great Depression. If you compare the charts of the rise and fall of the 1997-2000 NASDAQ and the 1929-1932 markets, they are eerily similar.

So why have I spent so much time talking about the NASDAQ when this is supposed to be a book about microcaps, OTCBB, and Pink Sheet stocks? Well, most of the investors that fueled the growth of the OTCBB came from the NASDAQ. As these investors lost their shirts in the larger markets, they disappeared from high risk penny stocks faster than documents at an Enron shredding party. In the years following the crash of the NASDAQ, OTCBB daily trading volume fell almost 85% and the market was set back nearly seven years to levels not seen since 1995. Investors were in a defensive mode and high risk stocks were O-U-T! Fewer investors meant little volume. Little volume meant wider spreads. Wider spreads led to even fewer investors. It was a viciously perpetuating cycle.

For all intensive purposes, the markets for penny stocks were dead. Message board traffic dried up, penny pick newsletters vanished, and penny stock websites went AWOL. Of the hundreds of websites and newsletters that I had listed in an appendix of my previous book, virtually all of them are now gone. Sad to say, I too closed my penny stock website. Sensing the end was near, I was fortunate enough to sell my website before the penny stocks completely went in the doldrums. As the penny stock websites disappeared, so too did MOMO plays, gappers, and various other trading strategies unique to that period of time.

Though it was only a shell of its former self, the OTCBB still traded over fifty four million dollars per day at its low point following the crash of the NASDAQ. The penny stock market was on life support, but over the past few years it has begun to show signs of life. We will examine the recovery of the OTCBB in the next chapter.

2

RESURECTION

In 2002, times were bleak for penny stocks. Venture capital for most OTCBB/Pink Sheet companies had dried up and the number of stocks quoted by these services had declined exponentially. There was little interest in these stocks among individual investors and message traffic on the bull boards was barren. It was as if a giant tsunami had washed the penny stock market clean. In hindsight, I feel that this was a good thing. In its heyday, the penny stock market was full of unscrupulous characters, many of whom ran dubious newsletters and websites that preyed upon investors that were new to the OTCBB and Pinks. As the markets faltered, many of these novice investors shunned volatile penny stocks and turned to more conservative investments. Without naïve newbie investors to prey upon, the nefarious perpetrators that ran many of the penny stock websites lost their target audience. As they no longer had anyone to manipulate, many penny stock websites and online newsletters went the way of the dinosaur. Other unsavory sites were eliminated when the Securities and Exchange Commission (SEC) stepped up its monitoring for online securities fraud. In 1998, the SEC formed its

Office of Internet Enforcement (OIE) to administer and handle the triage and investigation of enforcement-related leads generated from investor tips. As their resources grew and the number of penny stock tout sites decreased, the OIE had time to focus on major offenders. If you have some free time, check out the internet related litigation announcements on the SEC website. The page contains interesting reads about pump and dumps, stock manipulations, and other dastardly securities violations. Knowledge is power and knowing how these scoundrels work will make you a better investor. The elimination of these devious characters allowed the OTCBB and Pink Sheets to have a "fresh start", free from many of the manipulative practices that once plagued the penny stock market.

As market conditions for the broader indices improved in 2003, investors began to trickle back to the OTCBB. The allure of fast paced high potential investments was just too great for many to pass. By 2003, OTCBB average daily dollar trading volume had nearly tripled that of the previous year. 2004 built on those gains achieving a sharp increase for capital investment in OTCBB stocks. Gains were tempered somewhat in 2005 as January through May had a general downtrend on the broader indices.

Take a few minutes to compare the charts of the NASDAQ to the OTCBB dollar volume statistics. The OTCBB website http://www.otcbb.com contains data on market statistics for the over the counter market. In the market statistics subheading, you can find information on share volume, dollar volume, total transactions, etc. I personally don't like the charts provided on the OTCBB website, so I download the data into an excel spreadsheet. This allows me to create various charts for comparison and analysis of market trends. When looking at OTCBB market data, I like to look at total dollar volume to get a feel for overall market conditions. Dollar volume lets me know the "pulse" of the market. It is *real* data. Total share volume can be misleading because you don't know the price at which most tradable OTCBB stocks are moving. For example, a one cent stock may trade 20 million shares in a single day, but that only translates into $200,000…chump change for most large market stocks. Look at the chart in figure 1. Notice that the share volume increases dramatically while the dollar volume makes only modest gains. This find brings some interesting information to light. At first glance, it looks as if activity in the OTCBB is ramping up substantially. That is, things appear that way if you only look at the share volume. If you look at the dollar volume, you will see that the market has seen modest gains, but nothing close to the dramatic escalation in total share volume. The bottom line is how much cash is entering the market. More investors mean more money entering the market. More investors and more money means that more stocks are going to move. More stock movement means more opportunity for trading activity. Can you see the value of monitoring total dollar volume?

Comparing the dollar volume to the share volume in figure 1, it is apparent that tradable stocks on the OTCBB are changing hands at reduced prices. While total share volume has increased substantially, total dollar volume has not seen commensurate gains. The dollar stats tell the real story…that *real* activity in the OTCBB has increased modestly. While not earth shattering, this is nonetheless a good sign. Additionally, stocks trading at lower prices means more opportunity for big gains. Others would argue that stocks trading at lower prices means that the stocks are taking a beating and are at lower prices for a reason. That assessment may be true, but that is not what I am looking at.

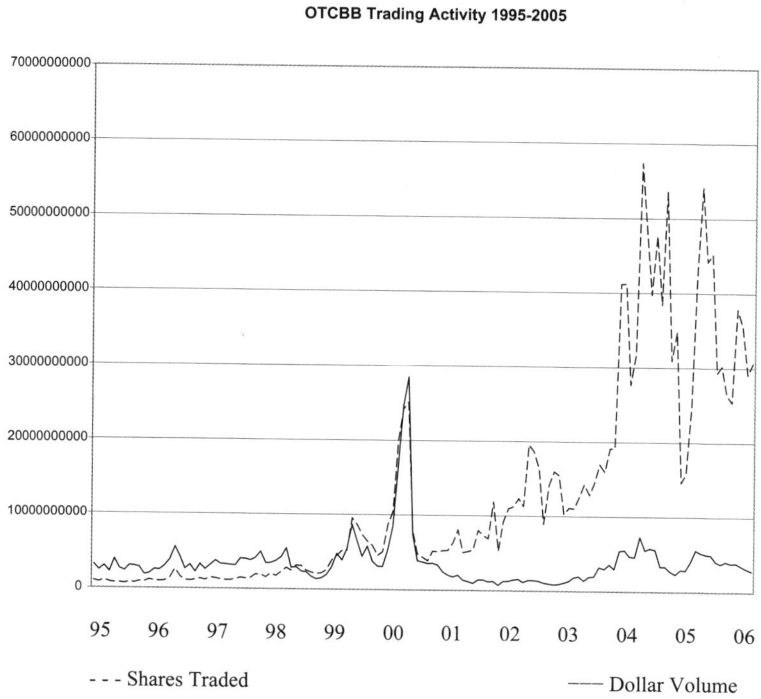

Figure 1: OTCBB Trading Activity from 1995 – 2006 comparing total share volume to total dollar volume. Note the sharp spike in activity at the early part of 2000. This was the "last hurrah" prior to the bursting of the internet bubble. As the OTCBB market crashed along with the broader indices, note how the total share volume dramatically increases while total dollar volume does not.

What interests me is market activity. Heavy market activity leads to high stock turnover. In order to trade a stock you need volume. That is an important point that I want to stress. There is a difference between *trading* and *investing* and I feel that both have a place in your portfolio. In my opinion, your long term retirement funds should be *invested* and we will discuss how to incorporate microcaps into your investments later in this text.

Trading is an activity that you should use more disposable funds for, especially when trading penny stocks. This is not a place for your nest egg! Rather, OTCBB and Pink Sheet stocks are something that you can line your nest with.

From my years of observing the markets, I am convinced that the majority of OTCBB and Pink Sheet investors come from NASDAQ minded individuals. This makes sense as those who invest in the NASDAQ tend to be tolerant of stock volatility and more apt to invest in lesser known equity securities. If you compare charts from the NASDAQ and OTCBB you will see that OTCBB activity tends to parallel NASDAQ activity (see the charts in figures 2 and 3). As I have postulated before, when times are good on the NASDAQ, it is my belief that investors often take some of their profits and stick them in OTCBB stocks. This was clearly evident in 1999-2000 and may be happening again now. As I am writing this book, the NASDAQ is approaching levels that have not been seen since 2001. When the NASDAQ made steady gains for the majority of 2003, dollar trading volume for the OTCBB followed suit a few months later. Again, it is my belief that most investors first make their money on the NASDAQ and then stick some of it in the OTCBB...hence the delay between activities amongst the two markets.

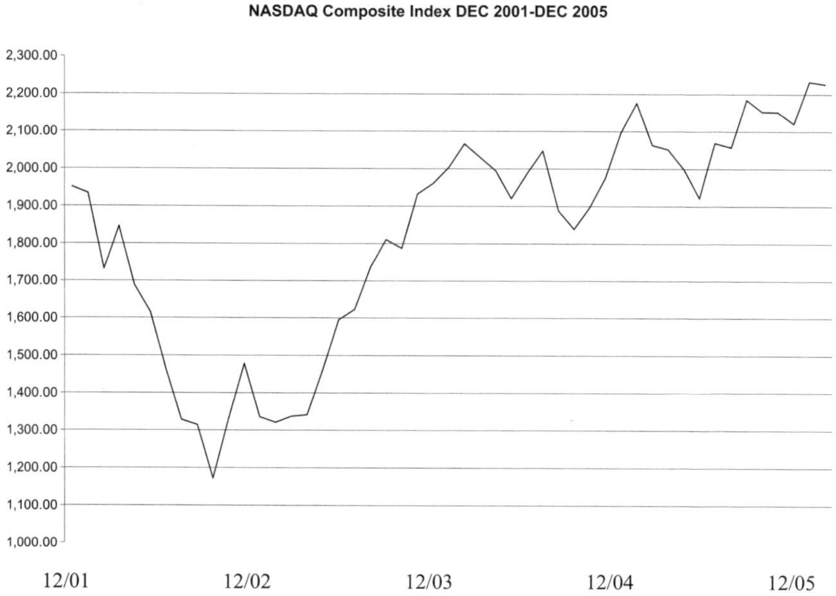

Figure 2: NASDAQ Composite Index closing prices from December 2001 to December 2005. Compare figure 2 to figure 3, the dollar volume of the OTCBB form December 2001 to December 2005 and note the similarities.

- ~11/02 – 1/04: NASDAQ rises
- ~12/02 – 1/04: OTCBB Dollar Volume rises

- ~1/04 – 9/04: NASDAQ falls
- ~1/04 – 10/04: OTCBB Dollar Volume falls

- ~9/04 – 1/05: NASDAQ rises
- ~10/04 – 1/05: OTCBB Dollar Volume rises

- ~1/05-5/05: NASDAQ falls
- ~1/05 – 12/05: OTCBB Dollar Volume falls

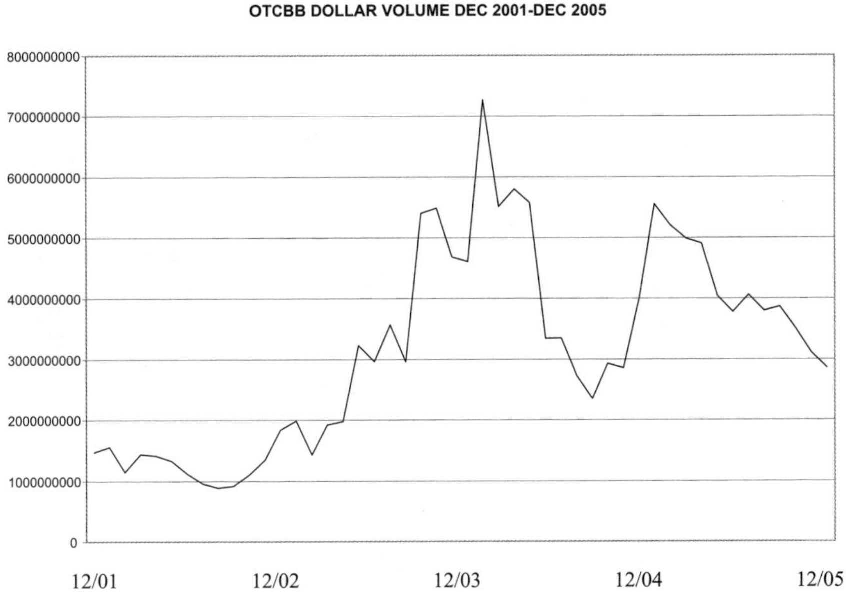

Figure 3: OTCBB Dollar Volume December 2001 – December 2005. Compare this chart to the chart in figure 2 on the previous page. Note the similarities that exist. Without a doubt, OTCBB dollar volume parallels NASDAQ trading activity. This information can be a useful tool in determining when to buy and sell OTCBB securities.

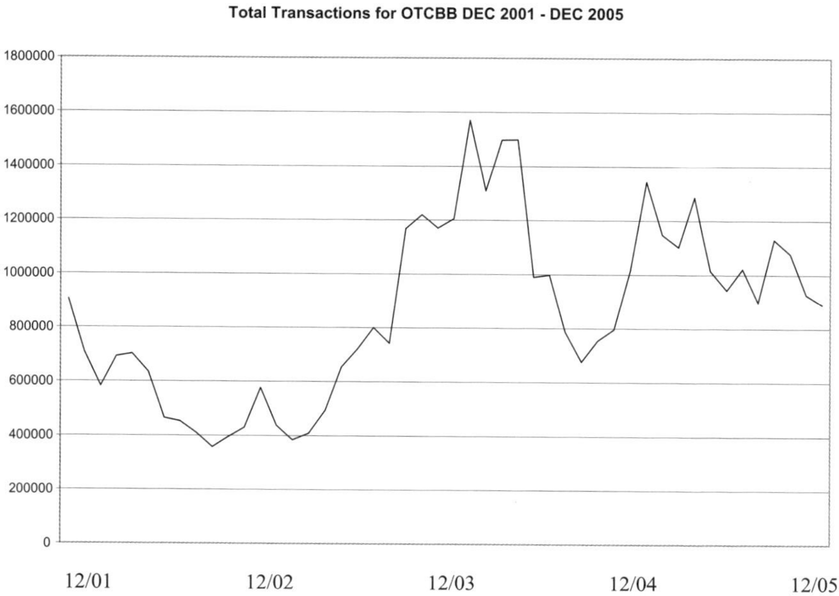

Figure 4: Total Transactions for the OTCBB Market from December 2001 – December 2005. Note the parallels to the NASDAQ. When the NASDAQ rises, transaction volume usually does the same after a short delay. Also compare this chart to the chart in figure 3, Total Dollar Volume for the OTCBB from December 2001 – December 2005. Again, note the parallels. An increase in total dollar volume coupled with an increase in transaction volume is a very positive sign for penny stock investors. These statistics indicate that activity is heating up for OTCBB stocks. An influx of cash into the market creates conditions conducive for trading stocks, hence the increase in transaction volume.

While OTCBB dollar trading volume gains tend to lag slightly behind gains in the NASDAQ, decreases in the NASDAQ influence the OTCBB much faster. When times are bad, investors tend to eliminate their riskiest investments first. As such, if the

NASDAQ is declining, the first things to go for most investors are their OTCBB investments. This trend was clearly evident for most of the year 2005. From January to May of 2005, the NASDAQ took a breather and experienced a general downtrend. As this occurred, investors likewise withdrew from the OTCBB and dollar trading volume declined. From May to July of 2005, the NASDAQ once again surged upwards and, as expected, OTCBB dollar trading volume began to follow suit. Unfortunately, just as the OTCBB began its positive dollar volume run, the NASDAQ once again corrected and the OTCBB rally died. From August to October of 2005, the NASDAQ experienced a minor correction and the OTCBB subsequently lost dollar volume. In general, 2005 OTCBB dollar volume was mired in a downward trend generated from the January-May and August-October NASDAQ corrections.

It is well known that the markets are very cyclical in nature and my observations of the parallels between the NASDAQ and OTCBB can create opportunities for "timing" investments in bulletin board equity securities. For example, from November 2005 to mid-April 2006, the NASDAQ enjoyed very substantial appreciation in value. In December of 2005, I noted that the NASDAQ was in the second month of a positive run and I expected the OTCBB to soon follow suit. The OTCBB hit a low point in dollar trading volume in December 2005 and then recovered explosively. From its December 2005 low to early April of 2006, dollar trading activity for the OTCBB improved by nearly 150%! When this occurred, a number of bulletin board stocks experienced amazing gains. As a matter of fact, a number of OTCBB stocks achieved quadruple digit percentage gains!

By the time you read this book, the dates I have just mentioned may be old news, but that is not important. The point I am trying to stress is that OTCBB activity tends to parallel that of the NASDAQ. Use this information to your advantage! People always ask, "How do you determine when to buy and sell a penny stock?" Well, this is one way to do it, especially if you are swing trading. If you see the NASDAQ in an extended downward trend, you can be fairly confident that activity on the OTCBB will soon do the same. Less activity will lead to less volume. Less volume will lead to wider spreads. Wider spreads will make a stock even more difficult to trade. Investors will get spooked and try to sell in an effort to conserve profits or cut their losses. This will drop prices even further. The stock will eventually level off as activity slows to a trickle. Very discouraging to say the least. For the shrewd investor willing to accept some risk, now may be the time to load up on cheap shares. It is a fairly common trading strategy. Some call it "bottom feeding" while others refer to it as "blood in the streets." It seems almost contrary to popular thinking…while everyone else is selling you are buying. For those of you that watch Seinfeld, you know that doing the opposite of what's expected once worked wonders for George Costanza. Eventually, the NASDAQ is going to recover, and when it does, history shows that the OTCBB tends to follow suit a short time later. When NASDAQ profits make their way back into OTCBB stocks, you can expect activity to rise, volume to increase, spreads to shrink, and prices to escalate. If you were brave enough to pick up shares when times were bleak, you will be sitting pretty.

So, is now a good time to return to the OTCBB? My opinionated answer to this question is a resounding "yes!" Statistics show that OTCBB dollar volume is increasing and prices are cheap. If you eliminate the anomalous activity of January to March 2000, you will see that the OTCBB dollar volume has recovered from the bear market and is approaching levels similar to those of the early internet boom. As the NASDAQ is currently experiencing a nice recovery and achieving highs not seen since early 2001, we can expect OTCBB dollar volume to continue improving as NASDAQ profits trickle to the over the counter market. While I don't tend to invest in Pink Sheet stocks as much as OTCBB stocks, there is money to be made in the pinks as well. In general, what holds true for the OTCBB stocks also holds true for pinkies.

Is the penny stock market fully recovered to its former glory of the internet boom? No, of course not. But then again, neither is the NASDAQ. The NASDAQ has fought and struggled its way back to 2,300+, a far cry from its heyday of 5,000. If the NASDAQ is having that much trouble reaching one half of its former high, you can't expect the penny stock market to be fully recovered. In all honesty, we may never again see times like 1999-2000. The internet was a new technology that fueled a once in a lifetime market. Though we are just a few years past this phenomenon, times and market conditions have changed drastically. As far as penny stocks are concerned, the market is cleaner, the risk of fraud has decreased, and potential for astronomical gains still exists.

3

TYPES OF MICROCAP STOCKS

You have no doubt heard of the term microcap stock, but what *exactly* does it mean? Over the years I have seen many definitions for a microcap stock. Some consider a microcap to be any stock with a market capitalization of less than five hundred million dollars. Others consider microcaps to have a market capitalization of less than three hundred million dollars. The SEC provides a fairly vague description as it states that the term microcap applies to companies with low or "micro" capitalizations. Logically, the term makes sense as "micro" infers a conceptualization of something small and "cap" makes reference to the company's market capitalization, or value of the stock multiplied by the total number of outstanding shares.

When you think of a microcap stock, you may automatically assume that this means the stock has a miniscule price tag; however, this may not be the case. For example, as I am writing this book there are nearly 700 stocks with a market cap equal to or less than $500 million and a share price greater than twenty dollars. Conversely, just because a stock has a tiny share price, it is not necessarily a microcap. Nortel Networks, for example, has a market capitalization approaching *$10 billion*, but its share price is just a few bucks. JDS Uniphase, one of the darlings of the internet bubble market, has a minuscule share price of just over $2.50 yet it has a market cap of *$4.25 billion!*

Since we are on the topic of assigning definitions to stock classifications, what exactly is a *penny stock*"? Again, like microcap stocks, there are many definitions for what is considered to be a penny stock. Some consider penny stocks to be any stock priced less than five bucks. Using that definition, Nortel Networks would be considered a "penny stock". It doesn't make much sense to call a $15 billion company a penny stock, does it? Some consider a penny stock to be any stock that trades at less than one dollar. That seems to make sense. If a stock is not worth at least a dollar, it is trading for change. Pennies are change, so the name seems to fit. Others consider a penny stock to be just what the name implies…a stock that costs pennies. I know plenty of people who consider 50 cents to be an "expensive" stock price. When these folks talk about a penny stock, they are generally talking about stocks that cost 10 cents or less.

When it comes down to it, a microcap or penny stock can be whatever you want them to be. Personally, I consider a microcap stock to be one that has a market capitalization up to $500 million and a share price less than 10 bucks. I consider a penny stock to be any security that trades for less than a dollar. While I very rarely trade them, I consider a subpenny stock to be exactly what its name infers…a stock that costs less than one penny.

So, where can you find microcaps, penny stocks, and subpennies? The answer is simple: you can find them everywhere! Microcaps stocks can be found on all exchanges. Yes, even the almighty New York Stock Exchange has microcaps. If you are looking for subpenny stocks, the Pink Sheets are the place to look. There are a ton of subpennies quoted by the Pink Sheets, with some stocks trading for as little as one hundredth of a cent! If you are looking for penny stocks, the OTCBB is the place to look. Currently, there are nearly 1,800 stocks trading at $1 or less on the OTCBB. According to the OTCBB, a penny stock is anything that trades for $5 or less. Going by that definition, there are nearly 2,400 penny stocks available on the OTCBB. If penny stocks are not your cup of tea, both the AMEX and the NASDAQ Small Cap Market are home to a cornucopia of microcap stocks. Let's take a more in depth look at the various places where you can find microcap stocks.

Pink Sheet Stocks

Pink Sheet stocks are commonly considered to be the most primitive of stocks in the evolutionary chain of equity securities development. The term "pink sheet" is a nostalgic term referring to days of old when information about these stocks was printed on, yes you guessed it, pink paper.

The Pink Sheets got their start back in 1904 when the National Quotation Bureau (NQB) began publishing daily and weekly lists of small securities that were traded over-the-counter. The pink lists published by the NQB contained the names of securities accompanied by contact information for the market makers that dealt with the stock. In order to trade a security, investors had to solicit quotes from three different market makers. Seems like a lot of work to make a simple trade! This scenario reminds me of the *Saturday Night Live* character "Grumpy Old Man" played by Dana Carvey back in the 1990's. If I close my eyes I can see the Grumpy Old Man saying, "You young kids today with your online trading, real-time stock quotes and whatnot…phooey! Back in my day, we got our stock quotes from moldy old pink sheets of paper. By the time we received the quote, the information was outdated and we usually paid the wrong price for the stock. That was the way it was and we liked it!"

Believe it or not, that just about sums up how pink sheet stocks were traded for decades.

All of this changed in the late 1990's thanks largely in part to one man…Cromwell Coulson. At one time, Mr. Coulson was a Wall Street trader that specialized in trading pink sheet stocks. His success with these stocks eventually allowed him to make an unprecedented move; he *bought* the Pink Sheets! In 1997, Mr. Coulson led a group of investors in the purchase of the NQB. Upon purchasing the bureau, Mr. Coulson wasted no time in making changes as he moved the company to the heart of New York's financial district and renamed the entity as the *Pink Sheets LLC*.

With the advent of online trading at the latter part of the last millennium, demand for a more efficient way to trade pink sheet securities pushed the Pink Sheets into the electronic age. In 1999, the Pink Sheets introduced the Electronic Quotation Service, an internet based quotation system allowing market-makers to publish real-time bids and offers for pink sheet securities. The implementation of this new quotation service opened the world of pink sheet investing to the common man. By eliminating the outdated quotation methods and the need to physically contact market makers in order to make trades, the newly created electronic quotation service allowed pink sheet investing to blossom. With current daily trading activity approaching $600 million, the Pink Sheets have certainly come a long way from their humble beginnings.

While the Pink Sheets LLC does provide information about certain OTC equities, it is not a regulatory commission, official exchange, or broker/dealer. According to the company website, "Pink Sheets is considered a Non-exclusive Securities Information Processor and an Interdealer Quotation System, for which registration is not required under current securities laws." Simply put, the Pink Sheets is a business. They provide a service and they get paid for such.

Pink sheet stocks are found on the over the counter market, or "OTC". OTC basically means that the stock is not listed on a major US exchange such as the NYSE, NASDAQ, or AMEX. Unlike OTCBB stocks which are required to report their current financial information to the SEC in order to meet eligibility requirements, Pink Sheet stocks do not have filing or reporting requirements. For companies, this can be a blessing as they do not have to spend valuable time or money preparing cumbersome financial reports for the SEC. For investors, the lack of financial filings makes it difficult to make an informed decision when performing due diligence on a potential investment.

Pink sheet companies fit many profiles. Some pink sheet companies are start ups with potential for unlimited growth. Others are large, well established foreign corporations such as Gucci, L'Oreal, Mitsubishi Corp., Nintendo, Foster's beer, Olympus camera, Peugeot, and Rolls Royce. A number of pink sheet stocks belong to large and well known companies that are in bankruptcy reorganization. As I am writing this book, companies such as Acclaim Entertainment, AMF Bowling, Ben Franklin Retail Stores, US Air, Gadzooks, Huffy, and Schlotzky's fit this profile. Some pink sheet stocks belong to companies that you know and love. Did you know that Conair, the maker of the hairdryer that is probably hanging in your bathroom, has stock that can be found on the pinks? How about Rent-a-Wreck? Solo-Serve? Gargoyles? Yep, they all belong to the pinks. (Well, they did at the time when I was writing this book…by the time you read it, things may have changed!) While I have mentioned a few of the stocks on the Pink Sheets that you have probably heard of at one point in time, realize that there are over 4,500 stocks quoted by the pink sheet quotation service.

Compared to stocks from the larger exchanges, pink sheet stocks have many advantages to offer. First of all, pink sheet stocks are typically cheap. In fact, some pinkies are downright ridiculously cheap! Would you believe it if I told you that some pinkies cost as little as $0.0001? It's true! For an investor with limited funds, pink sheet stocks afford the opportunity to accumulate a vast treasure-trove of shares. A second advantage of pink sheet companies is that they are often young start ups with potential for enormous future growth. Will you find the next Microsoft in its infancy? Probably not, but there is a chance that you may discover a solid company that eventually moves to a larger exchange or is acquired by another company at a premium price. A third advantage of pink sheet stocks is that they have the potential to appreciate very quickly. It is not uncommon for a pink sheet stock to rise thousands of percentage points in a matter of weeks. Want an example? Look at International Power Group, Ltd. (IPWG). As I am writing this book, the annual low for IPWG reached $0.03. Recently, this stock rose as high as $1.90 for a gain of over 6000%!

All of this sounds pretty nice doesn't it? Well, before you rush off to stick your kid's college funds into pink sheet stocks, let's look at some of the disadvantages associated with the pinks. First of all, as mentioned previously, pink sheet stocks are not required to report their financial data in order to be quoted. As such, you have no way of knowing what is truly going on with the company that you plan to invest in. Does the company have a legitimate business or is it simply a stock issuing operation run from a strip mall in Las Vegas? Second, pink sheet stocks have very limited access to media coverage. The only time many pink sheet stocks receive major media coverage is when they are involved in some sort of scandalous exposé. The limited media coverage of pink sheet stocks also leads to a third disadvantage: manipulative online profiling. In an effort to gain public exposure, many pink sheet companies are forced to utilize dubious online promotion services. These stock promoters often require companies to pay through the nose in the form of free trading shares in return for disseminating information about the company via mass emailings. If you look closely you will notice that most of these online stock promoters have disclaimers printed in micro-mini font full of legalese jargon and confusing syntax. Buried deep within the disclaimer you will almost always see a sentence such as, "we may hold positions in the companies that we profile and we may increase or decrease our positions in these companies at anytime." Basically, these folks are reserving the right to dump their free trading shares. This creates a problem. If the stock does happen to appreciate, a large dump of free trading shares from the promoters almost always kills the stock's run and individual investors are left holding the bag. Of course, not all online stock promoters fit this profile. But investor beware…there are a lot of bad guys out there. If you want some interesting reading, go to http://www.sec.gov and check out the "litigation release" section. Here you will discover a number of ways that people have tried to fleece unsuspecting investors. You will be very surprised at what you read.

Okay, let's get back to talking about disadvantages of the pinks. In the last paragraph, I mentioned that pink sheet stocks have the potential to appreciate very rapidly. While this is true, pinkies also have the potential to fall just as quickly. A stock that rises 200% one day may just as easily tank 75% in the ensuing trading session. Another disadvantage of the pinks is that many of the stocks are thinly traded. Some of these stocks can go for days without a single trade! Stumble upon one of these bad boys and you could be holding the stock for a long, long time!

With any investment, you have to balance risk versus reward. Pink sheet stocks take risk and reward to the ultimate extreme. That is why many financial advisors recommend that pink sheet stocks be avoided at all costs. If you are looking for a safe place to tuck away your retirement funds, the pink sheets are definitely not the place for you. If, however, you have a bit of cash that you can risk without breaking the bank, taking a chance on a pink sheet investment could yield amazing results. It is this potential that lures investors to the pink sheets. A typical trading day will produce a total dollar volume of nearly $600,000,000 for the pink sheets. While this amount is miniscule compared to the NYSE and NASDAQ, you must remember that many pink sheet stocks cost less than a penny. Considering this, the thought of over one half of a billion dollars exchanging hands on the Pink Sheets is quite amazing!

The best website for information on pink sheet stocks is http://www.pinksheets.com. This site is, of course, run by the Pink Sheets, LLC. If you are considering investing in the pinks, I highly recommend that you check this site out!

An Interview with the Chairman…

In January of 2006, I spoke to Cromwell Coulson, the current Chairman and CEO of the Pink Sheets LLC. Here is what he had to say:

Question: Mr. Coulson, as a young man, you were widely known for your prowess in trading pink sheet securities. What was it that attracted you to these stocks?

Mr. Coulson: I was attracted to the inefficiencies of these companies. There are many great companies listed on the Pink Sheets. Some of them just aren't as efficient as they could be. With some corrections, these companies could capitalize on their potential.

Question: What was the impetus that led to your purchasing of the National Quotation Bureau?

Mr. Coulson: Again, it was the inefficiencies that I saw. I saw an opportunity to move this quotation service forward.

And take it forward he did. Within a few years of purchasing the National Quotation Bureau, Mr. Coulson moved the company headquarters, changed the company's name, and began promoting the company to Wall Street executives. He eliminated the archaic paper trading system by implementing the Electronic Quotation Service (EQS), a JAVA technology based client application available over the web or a private extranet.

Question: Some have likened the Pink Sheets to the Wild West, referring to the "lawlessness and corruption" that seem rampant with these stocks. Are the Pink Sheets taking any steps to curb the fraudulent activity associated with its quoted stocks?

Mr. Coulson: We are not an exchange or a regulatory agency, so there is a limit to what we can do. The majority of stocks that dominate our daily dollar trading volume are respectable, legitimate companies. We are currently working on a "tier" system whereby we can separate the good companies from the bad. Companies that are large enough to list on major exchanges, that file audited financials, and hold annual shareholder meetings will be listed in our top tier. Companies will be charged a fee to be listed in our top tier and this will be another way to separate the good companies from the bad. Most of the bad companies won't have the funds for this service. The companies in our top tier will receive a template on our website to display financial data, post press releases, and so on. While we can't totally eliminate the bad companies from our quotation service, we can provide a service that focuses on the good companies.

Question: With new rules such as Sarbanes-Oxley, have you noticed an influx of companies from larger exchanges moving onto the Pinks?

Mr. Coulson: Yes. Sarbanes-Oxley was cost prohibitive for many companies. As a result of this, we have seen many of these companies move their stocks to the Pink Sheets.

Question: When these larger companies moved to the Pink Sheets, did they express any desire to be distinguished from the more dubious stocks quoted by the Pinks?

Mr. Coulson: Yes, some of them have. That is one of the reasons why we are proposing the tier system. We want to highlight the good companies.

Question: What do you see as the biggest problem facing Pink Sheet stocks?

Mr. Coulson: One of the biggest problems we face is guys with restricted stock from private placements or company insiders who sell restricted stock but they can't deliver the shares because of the restrictions.

Question: So, there are people selling restricted shares without filing a Form 144?

Mr. Coulson: Exactly.

Question: What about naked shorting?

Mr. Coulson: There aren't that many naked short sellers that spend their day crushing a stock. While it has received some press, there isn't much going on. The real problem is the undisclosed sale of restricted shares.

Question: Some have called the Pink Sheets the "Las Vegas" of the stock market. Do you agree with this assessment?

Mr. Coulson: That depends. There is a large variety of stocks quoted on the Pink Sheets. The better companies pose a high risk/high reward situation. The dodgier companies pose a high risk of separating you from your money.

I must say that I thoroughly enjoyed my conversation with Mr. Coulson. It is apparent that he is exercising great diligence and commitment to improving the Pink Sheets. Should the implementation of the tier system be successful, investing in Pink Sheet stocks will be a safer and more reliable proposition.

> (UPDATE: APRIL 2006) In mid-March 2006, the Pink Sheets LLC announced the implementation of their OTCQX premium listing service for OTC securities. OTCQX aims to promote OTC companies with strong fundamentals that are transparent in disclosure of their financial and operational data. According to the Pink Sheets LLC, the OTCQX trading platform will feature two distinct tiers, PremierQX and PrimeQX. PremierQX is the highest tier, identifying issuers that are of the size and quality to be listed on a National Stock Exchange, hold annual shareholders' meetings, and that have a minimum bid price of $1. PrimeQX is the second tier and identifies

those issuers that are operating companies with audited financials, but not of sufficient size to be on PremierQX. International companies quoted by the Pink Sheets will have the opportunity to participate in the OTCQX premium listing service as well. Every OTCQX listed company is required to meet exacting standards including:

- The posting of quarterly and annual financial reports on the OTCQX platform
- Interim disclosure of any relevant information that may affect share price
- Annual auditing
- Management disclosure and annual management certification
- 100 round lot shareholders
- Ongoing operations
    - This eliminates "shells" from participation in OTCQX
- Inclusion in the S&P or Mergent Manual, which satisfies the Blue Sky requirements for secondary transactions in many states
- International companies must be listed on a qualified foreign exchange and make their home country disclosure available in English

According to Pink Sheets LLC CEO Cromwell Coulson, "OTCQX is a viable, cost-effective and streamlined route to the equity markets that is an attractive alternative for many companies. By limiting OTCQX to operating companies with audited financials and professional advice, we believe the OTCQX premium tiers will provide a substantially better home for smaller companies that are currently considering listing on the AIM or OTC Bulletin Board. Moreover, admission to OTCQX is a way to join an elite roster of issuers that provide high quality disclosure to their shareholders. Foreign exchange-listed issuers will also find substantial advantages through our expedited disclosure process. The US equity markets remain the broadest and deepest in the world and OTCQX leverages the Pink Sheets' scalable quotation and trading platform that is used for all OTC stocks with nearly 200 participating broker-dealers."

The implementation of the OTCQX platform will effectively improve the safety of investing in pink sheet stocks. Companies that choose to participate in the OTCQX platform will meet requirements approaching the standards of large markets such as the AMEX or NASDAQ. I know what you are probably thinking…you are thinking, "If this is the case, why don't these companies simply choose to list on one of the larger exchanges?" I'll tell you why. The answer is Sarbanes-Oxley. The implementation of the Sarbanes-Oxley Act has become cost prohibitive for many companies. In order to list on the major exchanges or even on the OTCBB, companies must meet the requirements of Sarbanes Oxley. The OTCQX of the Pink Sheets allows companies that would otherwise likely list on larger exchange if not for the cost of complying with Sarbanes-Oxley to remain quoted in a respectable fashion.

Over the Counter Bulletin Board Stocks

The most active site for microcap investing is the generally thought to be the OTCBB. Technically speaking, the OTCBB is not an exchange. Like the Pink Sheets, the OTCBB is simply an automated quotation service for stocks that do not trade on a national securities exchange. Data provided by the OTCBB includes real-time quotes, last sales price, and volume information for OTCBB registered securities. According to the OTCBB, its tradable securities include national, regional, and foreign equities in addition to warrants, units, American Depositary Receipts, and Direct Participation Programs.

The OTCBB began operations in 1990 as a part of market reforms intended to provide transparency for Over the Counter securities transactions. The Penny Stock Reform Act of 1990 was a part of these reforms and mandated that the SEC establish an electronic reporting system to disseminate security quotations and last-sale data. Within a few years of the Penny Stock Reform Act of 1990, the OTCBB required firms to report trades of all domestic Over the Counter securities via the Automated Confirmation Transaction Service (ACT). The ACT is a computer system that matches trade information, determines locked-in trades, and submits them to clearing through the National Securities Clearing Corporation (NSCC). The ACT is the primary way that Over the Counter transactions in equity securities are reported. Participation is mandatory for all brokers that are members of a registered clearing agency and for all brokers who have a clearing arrangement with such brokers. Additional rules implemented by the OTCBB during this time included the 6600 rules series that required all OTC transactions be reported within ninety seconds of their occurrence.

The OTCBB is considered to be a step above the Pink Sheets because of the *OTCBB Eligibility Rule.* On January 5, 1999, the SEC approved the National Association of Securities Dealers's (NASD) proposed OTCBB Eligibility Rule, permitting only those companies that report their current financial information to the SEC, banking, or insurance regulators to be quoted on the OTCBB. The phase in for this rule began in July of 1999 and was completed in June of 2000. By the time this phase-in was completed, nearly 1,500 stocks were purged from the OTCBB. Today, there are just over 3,200 stocks quoted by the OTCBB. From its peak in 1998, the number of stocks quoted on the OTCBB has decreased by over 50%! Amazing, isn't it? Guess where most of these stocks ended up? That's right, they scurried over to the Pink Sheets.

The OTCBB Eligibility Rule provides investors with a measure of protection. In performing due diligence, investors in OTCBB securities have the opportunity to review the stock's SEC filings prior to making an investment. The OTCBB Eligibility Rule does provide said stocks with a measure of respectability compared to the pinkies, but that does not mean that they are not subject to manipulation. As mentioned in other chapters of this book, market makers for OTCBB stocks are notorious for failing to fill orders and then changing the bid/ask. This usually happens with thinly traded stocks. If a stock is hot with heavy action, there will usually be a number of market makers trading the stock. As such, you will generally have your order filled in a timely manner. Because the OTCBB does not have the more stringent listing requirements as those of the AMEX, NASDAQ, and NYSE, it tends to accumulate a number of companies that have a dubious nature. Many OTCBB companies are nothing more than press release machines. These companies will often make grandiose predictions, sign letters of intent, but they usually fail to deliver the goods. While pumping up investors with a false sense of security, company executives will sometimes dump their shares on the market. If asked why they are dumping shares, these folks often note that they do not receive a salary from the company and that their only form of compensation is from stock sales.

I know of one OTCBB "company", if that is what you want to call it, which has a very interesting track record. This particular company has had about a dozen different business plans over the years. Often, each business plan has nothing to do with the next. One year the company will be planning to open a casino and the next year it plans to enter oil exploration. The company often signs "letters of intent" and then usually fails to complete the transaction. This is a favorite ploy of many OTCBB companies. They enjoy touting their letters of intent. These letters often create excitement among investors and fuel trading in the stock. What investors fail to realize is that "letters of intent" don't mean squat. A letter of intent is not a binding contract. It simply means that both parties have discussed an option and reserve the right to act or not act upon said option. The company in question has had the same CEO for many years. He and his family members continually dump shares on the market while unsuspecting investors continue to trade the stock. Why, you ask, would people continue to invest in this stock if the CEO constantly dumps his shares? One word will answer your question…greed. Many OTCBB investors do not care about the company or the people behind the stock in which they invest. If the stock is cheap and has volume, it is tradable. If the stock is tradable, there is the potential to turn a profit. If people are making money, they don't really care what the CEO is doing. To be perfectly honest, the CEO of this company is not doing anything wrong. He files his Form 144's with the SEC indicating a planned sale of restricted stock. This information is available for all to see. If investors ignore proper due diligence and fail to see these multiple Form 144's, that is their problem.

The point that I am trying to make with this little tirade is that there are many OTCBB companies that are dubious at best. This is one reason why the OTCBB gets a bad rap in the investing community. I'll be the first to admit that there are a number of bad companies on the OTCBB. But, then again, there are also a number of good ones. The trick is to separate the good from the bad. The OTCBB Eligibility Rule empowers investors to make informed decisions about Over the Counter stocks. The fact that the pinks have no such empowerment places the OTCBB on a higher tier in the investment community.

> (UPDATE: APRIL 2006) On February 3, 2006, the Securities and Exchange Commission finally took steps to alleviate what many consider to be one of the biggest problems facing Over-the-Counter stocks. By approving amendments to Rule 3360, the SEC has expanded short interest reporting requirements to OTC equity securities. According to the amendments to rule 3360, OTC equity securities are defined as *any equity security that is not listed on the NASDAQ Stock Market or a national securities exchange.* With the amendments to rule 3360, members must maintain a record of total short positions in all customer and proprietary firm accounts in NASDAQ securities and OTC equity securities. Additionally, they must also report to the NASD

American Stock Exchange (AMEX)

In terms of trading volume, the American Stock Exchange (AMEX) is the third largest exchange in the United States, handling approximately 10% of securities traded in the country. The AMEX got its start in the early twentieth century as an alternative to the much larger New York Stock Exchange (NYSE). In the good ole days, brokers met at the curb outside of the NYSE and traded stocks that failed to list on the larger exchange. The action at the curb became so enormous that in 1921, the "curb exchange" moved indoors to a more respectable place of trade. At one time, the AMEX was the main rival to the NYSE. However, the recent emergence of the NASDAQ has somewhat diminished its role as an exchange powerhouse. Because of its more lenient listing requirements, the AMEX is heavily populated with microcap and smallcap securities. If you are looking for a safe and secure place to invest in microcaps, the AMEX is a good start. As you will soon see, the AMEX is often the first stop for stocks that graduate from the OTCBB.

NASDAQ Small Cap Market

The NASDAQ Small Cap Market contains stocks with small market caps that do not qualify for inclusion in the NASDAQ National Market. Stocks listed on this small cap exchange are still considered to be NASDAQ stocks and trade in exactly the same fashion as their larger counterparts. Like the AMEX, the NASDAQ Small Cap Market is a safe and secure place to find microcaps. As far as most investors are concerned, the NASDAQ, even if it is the Small Cap Market, has more prestige than the AMEX.

4

GRADUATION DAY

Most penny stock investors have a dream that their beloved stock will one day make the jump to the NASDAQ, AMEX or NYSE. I can't tell you how many times I have heard people say, "I'm gonna hold this stock until it reaches the NASDAQ. It's going to be worth $200 per share!" Just for grins, I recently cruised the bull boards to find some posts for validation. It did not take long to find such a post. DizzyXXX proudly predicted for the entire world to hear, "*Once we get to the AMEX our PPS will take off like a rocket!*" JDXXXTrader noted, "*Once we list on the AMEX, mutual funds and institutional investors will jump in. AMEX is a QUANTUM LEAP from the OTCBB!*" Okay, let's get real people. What is the rationale behind this thinking?

Just because your stock makes a jump to the major leagues, does this mean that your investment will yield larger returns? Better yet, what is the chance of an over the counter stock actually graduating to a larger exchange? To answer these questions, I analyzed OTCBB records from October 2004 to October 2005 for stocks that had moved on to greener pastures. Additionally, I went back a little further and checked the progress of other stocks that had made the jump a few years earlier.

In the timeframe I examined, there were 3,280 securities quoted by the OTCBB. Of these stocks, a total of 62 graduated to larger exchanges, thus producing a 2% graduation rate. To put it another way, there is a 98% chance that your stock will *not* move to a larger market over the next year. That is a sobering thought, isn't it? Now, if you were going to make a wager on whether or not your stock will make the jump to a larger exchange, where would you put your money? It's a no brainer! Of course, you would take the 98% bet. Despite the staggering odds, many investors stake their hopes and dreams on the 2% bet.

The thought sounds plausible enough…your penny stock moves to a larger exchange and it should bring you huge returns, right? Let me ask you this, have you ever owned a stock that moved from the pinks or the OTCBB to a larger exchange? Of all of the penny stocks that I have ever owned, I have only had a few that actually made it to a larger exchange. Although it happened quite a long time ago, I remember the first time that I had a stock graduate. When the stock finally made the long awaited announcement that it was moving to a larger exchange, I remember jumping for joy. My stock was headed for the AMEX. Personally, I was hoping for a move to the NASDAQ, but I was happy nonetheless. Okay, we were headed for the AMEX…finally, a "real" market for the stock. I was sure that it would take off. I figured that a move to the AMEX would give legitimacy to the stock, draw the attention of analysts, and make it available for mutual fund investment. Oh yeah…I was ready for the money to roll in! Guess what happened when my stock made the move to the AMEX. Nothing. Nada. Zip. That stock didn't do a darn thing! I could not believe it.

When this happened, my enthusiasm was crushed. I had always searched for *the one*, the one stock that would graduate from the OTCBB and make me rich. I finally found a stock that seemed to have it all. It had a reasonable float (for a penny stock), it was increasing its sales, and was turning a profit. Best yet, it was moving to a big exchange. Why didn't it move when it hit the AMEX? I ran this scenario over and over in my head. I just couldn't figure out what had happened. One day I finally thought to myself, "Who said that stocks would do great once they hit a large exchange?" The more I thought about it, the more I realized that I knew nothing about what a stock would do when graduating from the OTCBB. In my mind, I had assumed that the stock would do well. This sounds really cliché, but you know what happens when you assume.

Let's say that the stars and planets were correctly aligned and your stock announced that it was moving to a larger exchange. On which exchange would you expect your OTCBB stock to graduate? My analysis of OTCBB data from 2004-2005 indicates that of securities that moved to larger exchanges, 2% went to the NASDAQ, 8% went to the NYSE, and 90% went to the AMEX. So, odds are that your stock is headed for the AMEX. No problem. You are still ecstatic that your stock has finally made the move from the kid table to the adult table. Now, what type of performance should you expect from your stock now that it has moved to the big leagues?

Just as I had done in the past, most people assume that because a stock is being listed on a larger exchange, its price is going to magically skyrocket. I am going to show you that this is generally not true. By analyzing 30 stocks that jumped from the OTCBB to larger exchanges in 2004-2005, I noticed some interesting trends. First of all, in the six weeks prior to a stock being listed on a major exchange, an average appreciation of 22.7% was seen with extremes of 160% gains and 31% losses. Now, before you get too excited and rush out to scour the internet for stocks announcing moves to larger exchanges, listen to this interesting tidbit. On average, most companies only gave a few days notice prior to graduating to a larger exchange. I found a few instances where companies gave two weeks notice of their impending move to a larger exchange, but most companies only gave two days notice. Many times a company would give absolutely no notice that their stock was graduating. They would simply issue a press release stating that their stock was moving to said exchange effective immediately. Despite of the lack of pre-notification of the stock's impending graduation, it was interesting to note that six weeks prior to the stock moving to the larger exchange, there was often a significant increase in volume. Where did this volume come from? Could it be that investor speculation of a move to a larger exchange drove this volumetric push? Perhaps. I checked the message boards for many of these stocks and did indeed find rumors abuzz about moves to the AMEX, and NASDAQ. No one ever thinks that their stock is going to the NYSE and they always seem to hold their breath for the NASDAQ. I wonder why this is so? With only 2% of OTCBB stocks moving to the NASDAQ and 8% moving to the NYSE, it seems pretty obvious where the stock is going to go. That's right; most stocks are headed for the AMEX!

Why the AMEX you ask? To see where a stock is likely to end up if it graduates from the OTCBB, let's examine the listing requirements and fees for the various US securities exchanges. We will start with the AMEX. The AMEX has four different standards for the listing of domestic securities. For brevity, we will limit our discussion to the standard listing requirment. First off, in order to list on the AMEX, shareholders' equity in the applying company must be $4 million. Pre-tax income must be at least $750 thousand in the last fiscal year or in two of the last three fiscal years. There must be anywhere from four to eight hundred public shareholders and five hundred thousand to one million shares publicly held. The minimum price of the stock must be $3 and the market cap must be $3 million. The listing fees for the AMEX range from $35 thousand to $65 thousand depending on the total number of shares to be listed by the company.

Like the AMEX, the NASDAQ has multiple listing standards, but we will focus on requirements for listing on the NASDAQ Small Cap Market as this is the likely place for an OTCBB stock to end up if goes to the NASDAQ. For an initial listing on the NASDAQ Small Cap Market, a company must have stock holder equity of $5 million, a market value of $50 million, or net income of at least $750 thousand in two of the three prior fiscal years. There must be at least three hundred round lot shareholders with one million publicly held shares and a market valuation of at least $5 million for these shares. The company must also have three market makers and an operating history of one year. The fees for listing on the NASDAQ Small Cap Market range from $25 thousand to $50 thousand depending on the total number of shares to be listed by the company.

Listing requirements for the NYSE are much tougher than that of the AMEX or NASDAQ Small Cap Market. Yes, I know that you want to know why a higher percentage of OTCBB companies went to the NYSE over the NASDAQ if the NYSE has more stringent entry requirements. The OTCBB stocks that went to the NYSE in the timeframe that I examined were bank related stocks. These were not startups or small business, they were banks. Okay, enough about that. Let's get to the NYSE listing requirements. For an initial listing on the NYSE, companies must have anywhere from five hundred to two thousand total stockholders with at least one million one hundred thousand shares being publicly held. The company must have an average monthly trading volume of one hundred thousand shares for the most recent six months prior to listing. The company must have an aggregate market value of anywhere from $60 million to $100 million for publicly traded shares. Pre-tax earnings from continuing operations after adjustments for various items must total at least $10 million in the aggregate for the last three fiscal years together with a minimum of $2 million in each of the two most recent fiscal years and positive amounts in all three years. There are other valuation tests where the company can qualify for a listing if it has a global market cap of $500 million, $100 million in revenue for the most recent twelve months, and $25 million in aggregate cash flow for the last three fiscal years with positive amounts in each year. The fees for listing on the NYSE are based on the total number of shares to be listed and are comparable to that of the AMEX and NASDAQ.

Wow, those standards are pretty tough compared to the listing standards of the OTCBB. Hmm, what are the listing standards for the OTCBB? Have you ever thought about it? Let's take a look, shall we? According to the OTCBB, they are not a market or an exchange. The OCTBB is simply a quotation service for NASD market makers and, therefore, has no listing requirements. There are no financial requirements and there is no minimum bid price requirement. In fact, the only requirements for quotation by the OTCBB is that the company be registered with the Securities and Exchange Commission and be current in its filings with said agency. When you stop to think about it, quotation by the OTCBB seems rather simple. Let me assure you that it is not. I know a few CEO's that have waited up to two years for quotation approval by the OTCBB. It is amazing to think that after amendments to NASD Rule 6530 went into effect, nearly 50% of companies quoted on the OTCBB could not meet their listing requirements!

Now that we know what it takes to be quoted by the OTCBB, let's take a look at quotation requirements for the Pink Sheets. To be quoted on the Pink Sheets, a company needs to find one market maker that is willing to quote their stock. That's it! The Pink Sheets note on their website that over two hundred market makers participate in trading pink sheet stocks and they even furnish a link that provides information on how to contact these market makers. There are no listing requirements to be quoted on the Pink Sheets and issuers are not required to pay any fees. Once listed, the Pink Sheets does not have a requirement that the issuer continue to provide updated financial information. Federal law, however, does require that "adequate current information" be publicly available when an issuer's securities are trading under certain circumstances. When you look at the requirements for pink sheet stocks even, the OTCBB looks pretty stringent. Just about anyone with a little cash can have a stock listed on the pink sheets. All you need to do is hire a market maker to file a form 211.

> (UPDATE: APRIL 2006) The new OTCQX trading platform offered by the Pink Sheets LLC has very strict requirements that rival those of the larger exchanges. Please refer to pages 31-33 for more details.

I got into this discussion on listing requirements because we were discussing where a stock would most likely move if it was to graduate from the OTCBB or Pink Sheets (see figure 5). History shows us that Pink Sheet stocks usually graduate to the OTCBB, OTCBB stocks usually graduate to the AMEX, and AMEX stocks usually graduate to the NASDAQ. Last, but not least, a few NASDAQ stocks move to the NYSE. This is usually done as a matter of prestige as the NYSE is considered by many to be the world's top securities exchange.

Pink Sheets → OTCBB → AMEX → NASDAQ → NYSE

Figure 5: Typical progression of stocks quoted and listed on US securities exchanges. The Pink Sheets and OTCBB are not technically exchanges as they merely serve as quotation services for NASD market makers.

Chances are, unless you were already in the stock that is making a move to a larger exchange, you are not going to be able to take advantage of the stock's appreciation in the six weeks leading up to its graduation. Even if you were already invested in the stock in question, you would not officially know about the move to the larger exchange until a few days before it happened as companies typically wait until the last minute before announcing their moves. When you did hear this news, what would you do? If you are like everyone else, you would jump for joy, add more shares to your position, and wait for the stock to skyrocket once it hit the bigger exchange. Well guess what? If your stock behaves like most others, you are in for a big surprise. What happens when a stock makes the jump you ask? First of all, in the initial six weeks following a move from the OTCBB to a larger exchange, stocks fell an average of 5% from the closing price just prior to the graduation date and had a corresponding decrease in volume. Extremes of an 82% gain and a 42% loss were also noted during the six week post jump period.

For many, the results of this six week period will create confusion and despair. The excitement of the pre-graduation escalation quickly fades and reality sets in. What happened? Investors were expecting many things after their stock graduated to a larger exchange, but a 5% loss and dramatic drop in volume were not what they had in mind. A number of investors will sell their positions and move on to other stocks. This is reflected in the stock's activity following the initial six weeks after graduation.

On average, stocks hit their lows one to four months after jumping to a larger exchange, falling an average of 33% from their graduation price. In fact, of the thirty stocks analyzed, only two managed to never fall below their graduation price. This means that there is a 93% chance that your stock will drop in value following its move to a larger exchange. Extremes found during this timeframe were a gain of 11% and a loss of 70%. So, according to my analysis of thirty stocks that graduated from the OTCBB to larger exchanges from October 2004 to October 2005, you have a 7% chance of making a maximum gain of 11% and a 93% chance of taking a bath of up to 70% in the first three to four months following your stock's graduation to a larger exchange. Not good.

Don't lose heart just yet my friend. Further analysis of these stocks showed that six months after graduating to a larger exchange, these stocks ended up 1-2% above their graduation price. "So what?" you say. What is so great about a 2% gain after holding a stock for so long? What about the triple digit gains that were supposed to accompany the move to a larger exchange? Before we continue, let's get one thing straight. In most cases, there are no immediate astronomical gains when a stock graduates from the OTCBB. Let's put an end to that ill conceived thought right here and now. Instead, rather, let's focus on how we can use this new knowledge to our advantage. For starters, the results of my analysis strongly suggest selling and taking a profit when a stock graduates to a larger exchange. According to my analysis of the graduated OTCBB stocks for 2004-2005, there was a 93% chance that you would lose money in the ensuing three to four months if you held your position. If you chose to take a profit upon graduation, it would then behoove you to closely monitor the stock and consider retaking a position during the next three to four months. During this timeframe, graduated stocks lost an average of one third of their pre-graduation value. Can you say blue light special? We also know that by six months following graduation, these same stocks settled at 1-2% above their pre-graduation value. If everything panned out according to the averages, there is an opportunity for a quick 35% gain! The key is timing and we all know that no one has the *exact* answer for that.

Of course, by trading stocks in this manner pre and post graduation, there is a small chance that you could miss out on a big winner. Cuisine Solutions (AMEX: FZN) for example, rose 73% in the six months after its graduation from the OTCBB and never fell below its jump price. (Just in case you were wondering, FZN was not one of the thirty stocks included my analysis) On the other hand, you could make out like a bandit! Sinovac Biotech Ltd. (AMEX: SVA) rose 22% in the six week pre-jump period only to fall 58% after graduation. By six months after graduation, SVA had risen back to nearly 60% above its pre-graduation price! Predictably calling tops and bottoms in the market is virtually impossible, so it would be wise to set your own personal entry and exit points for these stocks. I have shown you the averages. I have given you the timeframes in which these stocks typically rise, fall, and then rise again. Again, remember that these were *averages* for thirty graduated OTCBB stocks during a one year timeframe. Not all stocks are going to behave this way.

Figure 6 depicts a typical situation for a graduating OTCBB stock. Transmeridian Exploration (AMEX: TMY) graduated from the OTCBB to the AMEX on March 21, 2005. Note that beginning in February, approximately six weeks prior to graduation day, Transmeridian stock began to increase in value. On March 21, 2005, the first circle on the left of the chart, the stock graduated from the OTCBB to the AMEX. Note that in the initial six weeks after graduating, TMY experienced a steady decline and dropped even further after that. TMY hit its low point about two months after graduating from the OTCBB. From this point, TMY had a slow and steady recovery. TMY finally regained its graduation price nearly six months after making its move from the OTCBB to the AMEX. After reaching this break even point, TMY stock has taken off like a rocket!

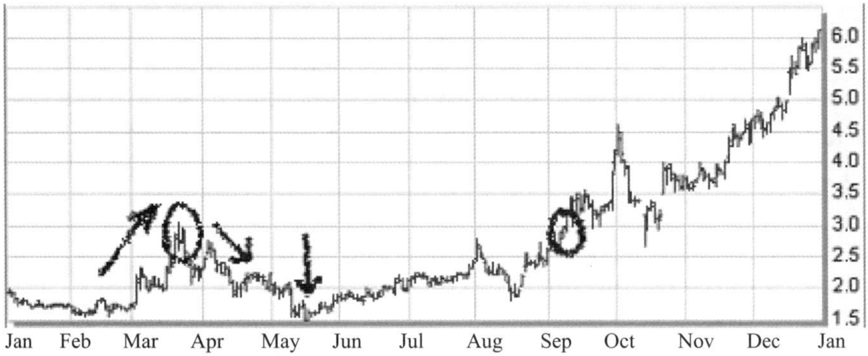

Figure 6: TMY 1 year chart
TMY graduation from the OTCBB to the AMEX is depicted by the first circle on the left of the chart. Note the pre-graduation run (1st arrow). Also note the initial price drop typically seen in the first 6 weeks following graduation (2nd arrow). As some investors become frustrated with the stock's lack of performance after graduating to a larger exchange, they sell their positions creating a second price drop (3rd arrow). Approximately 6 months after graduation, the stock finally eclipses its graduation price (2nd circle).

Not all stocks follow the pattern that I described in this chapter. Remember that what I described were averages. I used the TMY chart because it is very close to the averages that I described. While the chart is close to the averages, it does not fit them perfectly. What I do like about this chart is that it clearly shows the pre graduation run-up and the two phase price drop following graduation. TMY hit its low point a little early at two months after graduation. Most other graduated stocks hit their low points two to four months after graduating from the OTCBB. As described in this chapter, approximately six months after graduating, TMY finally eclipsed its graduation price.

5

SUBPENNY STOCKS

No book on microcap or penny stock investing would be complete without a mention of subpenny stocks. Typically found on the Pink Sheets and occasionally on the OTCBB, subpenny stocks are just what their name implies…stocks that trade at prices less than one cent. So, how can you make money on these stocks? I am often asked this question not only about subpenny stocks, but about penny stocks in general. What many people fail to realize is that it's not the *price* of a stock that makes or loses you money, it's all a matter of *percentages*. When many people think of stocks, they tend to think of higher priced conventional stocks such as those found on the NYSE. If one of these stocks advances in price by a penny or two, it is no big deal. On the other hand, if a two cent penny stock advances by two cents, it *is* a big deal. In fact, it is a very big deal. Such a situation nets you a 100% gain on your investment! Many people fail to grasp this concept.

For people that do grasp the concept of percentages, subpenny stocks are an attractive proposition because of their potential for fast and furious gains. Think about it, $60 NYSE stock advancing two cents is meaningless. A $20 NASDAQ stock advancing two cents is forgettable. An $8 AMEX stock advancing two cents is nothing to write home about. A fifty cent OTCBB stock advancing two cents is not a bad gain for a single day, but it is not going to make you rich. A two cent gain for a half cent stock, on the other hand, is enormous! But how realistic is it for a subpenny stock to advance two full cents in one day? To find out, let's take a more in-depth look at the world of subpenny stock investing.

To many, the thought of a stock trading for less than a penny is ludicrous. Honestly, how is it possible for a company to have shares of its stock trade for as little as one thousandth of a cent? Yes, you read that right...*one thousandth* of a cent! In today's economy, a single piece of gum costs a quarter, a call from a payphone will set you back thirty five cents, but it's possible to buy five thousand shares of a company's stock for a *nickel*? It may sound inconceivable, but it is true. So, exactly what kind of company has stock that trades for under a penny? To find out, I randomly examined some of the most actively traded subpenny stocks on the Pink Sheets.

On February 3 of 2006, CNES had 2.6 *billion* shares of its stock trade on the Pink Sheets. On that same day the total trading volume for the NYSE was 2.3 billion shares and the NASDAQ had 2.27 billion shares trade hands. Amazing, isn't it? What was it about CNES that compelled people to trade more shares in this one subpenny stock than the total trading volume for entire NYSE? According to their SEC filings, CNES has 8.95 billion shares outstanding, giving it a market capitalization of $2.7 million dollars. CNES has more outstanding shares than either Microsoft or Wal-Mart! SEC filings indicate that the company issued around

547 million new shares in 2004 and a whopping 5.6 billion new shares in 2005! Why were so many new shares issued? One reason for so many new shares is that the company reported a working capital deficiency of $2.8 million dollars. Such a reason for this situation may be the fact that the company has reported no revenue for the fiscal years ending September 30, 2004 or 2005. With a lack of working capital and no realized revenue, the company has been forced to issue new shares to finance its continuing operations. This is not an uncommon practice for most publicly traded stocks, but 5.6 billion shares issued in one year is pretty extreme.

A few other subpenny stocks I randomly examined were similar to CNES in the fact that they all traded a substantial number of shares in one day. QBID, for example, traded 1.7 billion shares on February 3, 2006. On that same day, PLNI traded 259 million shares and DDSI traded 216 million shares. While it was very easy to find information on CNES, performing due diligence for the other stocks was not quite as simple. Remember, Pink Sheet stocks are not required to file their financial data and many of them don't. When it comes to subpenny stocks, a majority of these stocks are not fully reporting. Considering this, I would like to commend CNES for filing their 10K's and 10Q's with the SEC. These documents make performing due diligence much easier and allow investors to make informed decisions when contemplating an investment. After spending an inordinate amount of time searching for information on QBID, PLNI, and DDSI, I gave up. I can only imagine how others feel when trying to perform research on these stocks.

When companies don't file with the SEC, it seems as if they have something to hide. When you combine this notion with the fact that most subpenny stocks have mounting debts, little revenue, and ever increasing floats, the word "shady" comes to mind. Although subpenny stocks make up only a small percentage of the 4,800 stocks quoted by the Pink Sheets, their dubious nature is often considered to be the impetus for the questionable reputation associated with the pinks. In fact, one prominent CEO told me, "Anyone who invests in stocks like that is a dumb #@%." I can't, in good conscious, write what he actually said just in case there are children reading this book! Let's just say that this particular CEO felt that anyone who invested in subpenny stocks was not very smart and that they deserved to lose their money.

Are all companies with subpenny stocks bad companies? I would venture to say no, not all of them. Some subpenny stocks have revenues in the millions of dollars and offer excellent products or services. Many of these companies are simply straddled with enormous debt and fall into a cycle of consistent share dilution in an effort to fund the ongoing operations. For example, GlobalNet Corporation (Pink Sheets: GLBT) is a company with $75 million in reported revenue and a share price of $0.0002. Over the past year, the company has issued millions of shares in an effort to raise working capital. In fact, during the last 10 months (Sept 2005 – Jun 2006) GLBT has filed over a half dozen Form 8K's with the SEC to announce sales of equity securities. Overall, sources indicate that GLBT has over 4 billion shares outstanding. Wow! Besides constant share dilution, other subpenny stocks may be in their current predicament due to a rash of naked shorting or other forms of stock manipulation. We will examine the situation of shorting microcaps in a later chapter of this text. Don't get me wrong, there are plenty of subpenny stocks that are questionable at best and there is often a reason why these stocks trade for less than a penny.

I must admit that I have purchased shares in subpenny stocks over the years. Believe it or not, I have actually made some nice profits from many of my subpenny trades. I liken investing in subpenny stocks to gambling in Las Vegas. By no means would I ever place any substantial amount of money into a subpenny stock.

Whenever I do purchase a subpenny stock, I always use cash that I am willing to lose. I do the same thing whenever I head to Vegas. I take a set amount of cash and anticipate losing it all. I know that the house has the edge and if I come away empty handed I have mentally prepared myself ahead of time. I simply consider my loss payment for entertainment. If, on the other hand, I happen to come away with a profit…all the better. I go into a subpenny investment knowing that it is highly likely that I may lose most of my money. Now, I know what you are thinking right about now. You are probably thinking, "If you plan on losing your investment, why invest there in the first place?" Simply put, the answer is subpenny profit potential. I have purchased subpenny stocks for $0.006 and sold them for $0.02 a short time later. A quick 200%+ gain is not bad in my book! It's almost like having your Ace painted with a face card while sitting at the blackjack table. If I do invest in a subpenny stock, which is very rare, I don't even bother researching the company. I know that chances are I won't find any credible information anyway, so I don't waste my time. Whenever I have a subpenny investment, it is purely a momentum play. If I notice a lot of buzz about a particular subpenny stock on the message boards and if I see a number of newsletters pumping said stock, I may take a small position and try to catch the wave. If I can make a few tenths of a cent on my investment, it could mean a large percentage gain. If not, I cut my losses and move on.

A great example of this scenario recently occurred with the stock of a New Jersey based biopharmaceutical company named Xechem International, Inc. (OTCBB: XKEM). In May of 2006, XKEM stock was trading for as little as $0.007. Despite the fact that the company had reported revenues of only $6 thousand, $4.5 million in debt, and nearly 1 billion outstanding shares, XKEM generated a great deal of hype during the month of June. Rumor had it that the company's flagship product was nearing approval for sale in a foreign country and a few penny stock newsletters/websites spread the word to the masses. Investors were obviously excited about this rumor as the stock experienced a surge in volume and a steadily increasing share price. In this short timeframe, the XKEM message board on Raging Bull received an astounding 40,000 posts! By early July, those who were willing to take a chance on the subpenny stock were duly rewarded as XKEM hit a high of $0.115. In just over one month's time, XKEM provided potential returns approaching 1500%! However, as is the case with most subpenny stock gains, these returns were short lived. A few days after hitting its high, XKEM began to fall and nearly half of those gains were erased. (see figure 7)

While many investors made money on the way up, those who were late to the XKEM party lost a substantial portion of their investment. When a stock makes significant gains, many people lose their common sense and assume that the stock is going to increase forever. On July 5, 2006 XKEM opened positively with a half cent gap to just over 9 cents. Investors were excited. XKEM had been moving north for nearly one month and during the week preceding July 5, the stock had appreciated at an even faster pace as a horde of new investors jumped on the XKEM bandwagon. This was evident as multitude of new posters appeared on the XKEM message board and postings nearly doubled to 2,000 posts per day. Shortly after 2:00pm, XKEM finally made the announcement that everyone had been waiting for…they had received approval to market and sell one of their products in Nigeria. This news instantly generated frenzied exuberance and the stock traded nearly 42 million shares over the next 15 minutes. Now, this is the part that leaves me scratching my head. Despite the fact that the stock had risen nearly 1500% in only one month, some investors were still assuming that the stock would continue to climb to ridiculous heights. One guy predicted 15 cents (a 30% gain from the newly established high and a 2042% gain from the recent low) while another predicted 25 cents (a 117% gain from the newly established high and a 3,471% gain from the recent low). One poster, giddy with excitement, said $1.25 was due (a gain of nearly 1000% from the newly established high and a 17,757% gain from the recent low). Come on people, let's get real. It is this type of thinking that gives penny stock investors a bad name. While many investors were irrationally chasing the stock as it spiked on news, a few investors had some common sense. One of the oldest adages in stock investing is to "buy on the rumor and sell on the news." In fact, one sage investor posted that exact message on the XKEM board within 10 minutes of the long awaited press release (probably after he sold, of course). While a majority of the board was patting each other on the back and shouting "TO DA MOON", the smart investors were taking their profits as fast as the market makers would process them. When they told others to sell, the board simply branded their former allies as bashers. Like clockwork, within 30 minutes of the press release, XKEM lost its post-news pop and the stock began to slide. As the stock fell towards the close, those who failed to sell were stunned with disbelief. One poster queried, "What is going on here? This is great news. Why are we falling?" Others began to panic and claimed that crooked market makers were naked shorting the stock. Just a few short hours after the XKEM press release, the stock had tumbled nearly 33% from its high of 11 cents to a close of around 7 cents. A few days later, the stock was down nearly 50%. (see figure 8)

Many investors will read the XKEM story and say, "You see, I told you so. Those penny stocks are pure @#$%!" To these naysayers, I would like to ask the following question: How many large cap stocks had gains of over 100% last year? The answer is that very few did. In fact, during an average year, most large cap stocks provide returns of less than 10%. Although XKEM's run was short lived, the stock did afford many investors the opportunity to achieve enormous gains. For that I say, "Bravo, XKEM!"

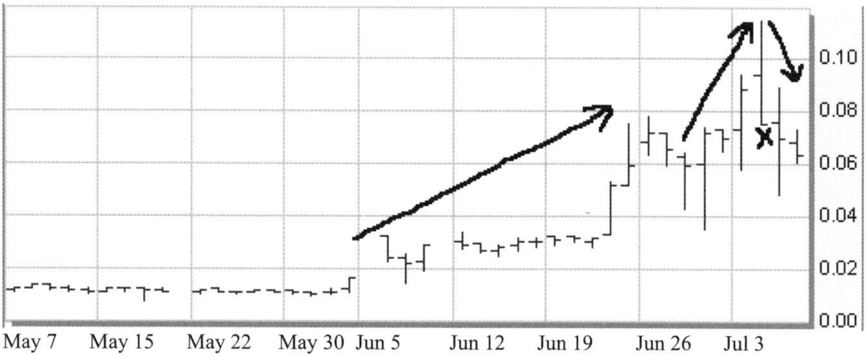

Figure 7: Two month chart for Xechem (OTCBB: XKEM). Note the two phased stock appreciation. Over the month of June 2006, XKEM began a steady rise as a number of websites and newsletters touted the stock. As the stock continued to rise, more investors jumped on the XKEM bandwagon, particularly in the week leading up to a long anticipated press release. This second phase of XKEM stock appreciation is noted by the second arrow. On Jul 5, marked by the "X", XKEM finally announced the press release that had been the focus of the prior month's hype. Note the precipitous drop in stock price immediately following the press release.

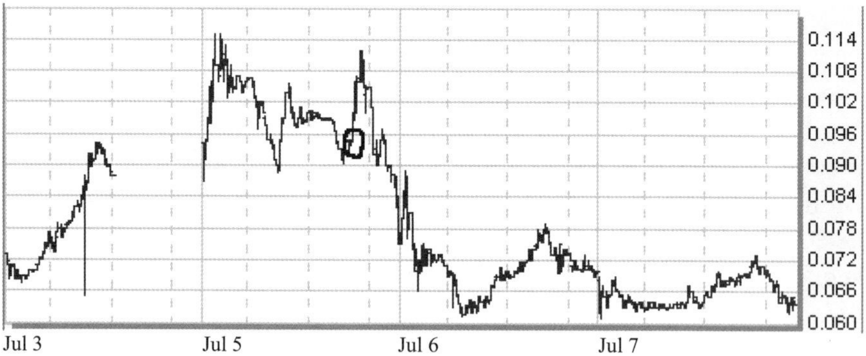

Figure 8: One week chart for Xechem (OTCBB: XKEM). The circle denotes the XKEM press release which occurred at 2:26pm on Jul 5. Note the sharp and immediate rise in stock price following the press release. This price spike was short lived. Within 15 minutes of the press release, investors began to sell on the news and the stock dropped nearly 33% from its post-news high. A few days later, the stock had dropped nearly 50%.

A second example of a subpenny stock providing amazing returns recently occurred with the stock AmeriResource Technologies, Inc. (OTCBB: AMRE). For those of you with good memories, you may recall that I mentioned this stock in my last book, *Penny Stocks: The Next American Gold* Rush. While the name of the company is the same as it was seven years ago, this stock has a new symbol, a new business plan, and now trades on the Pink Sheets. AMRE is a typical subpenny stock with consistently negative net income, substantial debt, and a constantly growing number of outstanding shares. Yeah, I know that those details sound pretty awful, but that is not important. Remember, with most subpenny stocks, you are not investing based on the merits of the company, you are making an investment based on momentum. For quite some time, AMRE sat relatively stagnant with a subpenny price approaching $0.004. Ah, now don't you just love it when you can buy two shares of stock for less than a penny? All of this changed when a single website began to pump AMRE. The website noted that they had purchased 12 million shares between June 30 and July 5 prior to their mentioning of the stock. After loading up on AMRE shares, this website recommended the stock as a "MEGA BUY" and the game was on. Seasoned penny stock investors suspected that this was a pump-and-dump. With all of the bad press that pump-and-dumps have received over the years, you would think that investors would avoid these stocks like the plague. Well, if you did think that you would be dead wrong. Within minutes of the "MEGA BUY" recommendation, AMRE stock traded 13 million shares. Within one hour of the recommendation, the stock traded nearly 76 million shares! So much for investors avoiding suspected pump-and-dump stocks. By the end of the day, AMRE stock had risen an amazing 190% on the heels of a simple recommendation by a single website. A few days later, the stock had climbed 900% from its $0.004 start. (see figure 9) Say what you will about subpenny stocks, but this type of action would never occur with a large cap stock. When a large cap stock receives an upgrade, it may jump 5%, but 900% is simply out of the question. Do you remember what I said about subpenny profit potential? Now you see what I mean. When it comes to subpenny stocks, it does not matter what the company is or does. The only thing that really matters with these stocks is momentum. Just look at AMRE! By the way, the website that was touting AMRE quit mentioning the stock a short time after its price spike. I wonder if they sold their shares. I know what I think, but I'll let you decide for yourself.

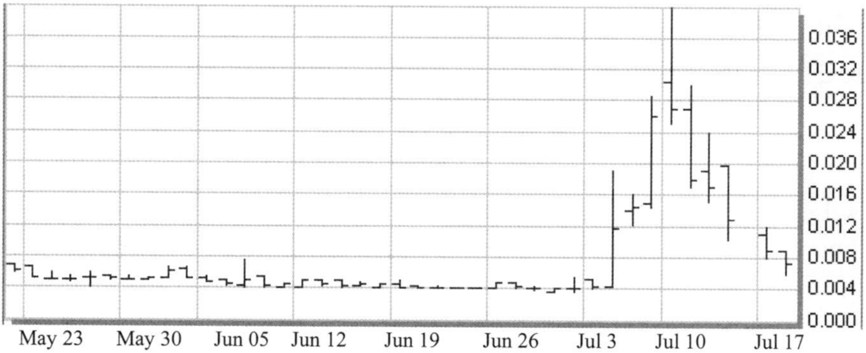

Figure 9: Two month chart for AmeriResource Technologies. Note that the stock sat relatively stagnant in the weeks prior to the "Mega Buy" recommendation that came out on July 5. Following the recommendation, note the immediate and substantial price appreciation for AMRE stock. This price spike was short lived, however, and the stock was back under a penny within a few weeks.

Believe it or not, a week or so after touting AMRE as a "MEGA BUY", the website in question quit mentioning AMRE and began to tout another stock. QTCE was the new play and the website noted that the company had given them 14 million free trading shares and 21 million restricted shares prior to their mentioning the stock. I guess those 35 million shares weren't enough because the website saw fit to spend a whopping $6,400 to purchase an additional 1.6 million shares on the open market. Despite the fact that many people were left holding the bag after their last pump job, this website once again succeeded in boosting the price of their target stock. On the day that QTCE was mentioned by this website, the stock hit an intraday high of $0.027 for a gain of over 400%! Not bad…if you sold on the way up that is! By the market close of the following trading session, the stock had tumbled back to $0.007. (see figure 10) If you had been foolish enough to buy this stock near its high, you would now be down nearly 75% in just one day!

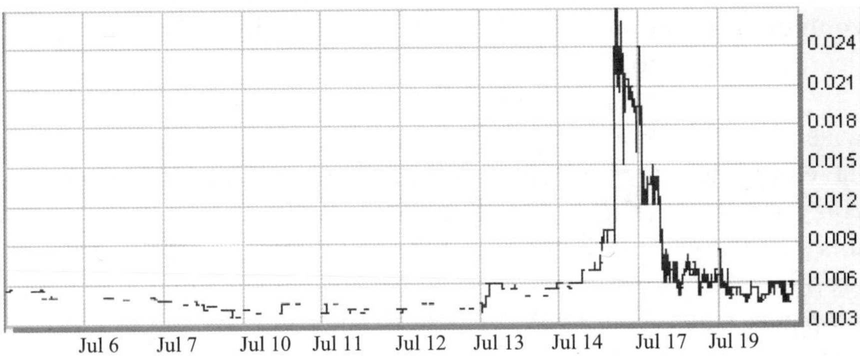

Figure 10: Two week chart for Quantech Electronics Corp. (Pink Sheets: QTCE). Note the massive price spike that occurred on July 14 in conjunction with a single website recommendation for the stock. By the end of the following trading session, this stock had lost nearly all of its gains. Talk about volatility!

While subpenny stocks may be considered the pariahs of the investing community, there is no doubt that they do offer the potential for amazing gains. If you do decide to invest in a subpenny stock, please be cognizant of a few things. First of all, some subpenny stocks rarely change in value. While it may appear that your stock is trading like gangbusters with volume approaching 100 million shares, your stock may have a float of a couple billion shares. While a 100 million share trading day would send most stocks through the roof, a 100 million share trading day for your 2 billion share stock barely puts a dent in the float. Additionally, an all too common consequence of these large floats is the reverse split. Some subpenny stocks routinely utilize reverse splits to temporarily elevate their share price and reduce the size of their float. In nearly every reverse split that I have ever seen, the investor gets the short end of the stick. Soon after the stock price rises from the reverse split, it often falls back to the levels where it previously dwelled. Now you are stuck back at the same old subpenny price and you have fewer shares to boot. In many cases, after the company has reduced the size of the float with the reverse split, they begin issuing new shares again in an effort to fund continuing operations. Can you say share dilution? Can you say decreased shareholder value?

Subpenny stocks can be a dangerous game. One would be wise to treat them as such. If you can accept the risk, these stocks have the potential to provide enormous returns. Remember the crazy action of XKEM, AMRE, and QTCE? If you choose to play this game, please be cognizant of the fact that these stocks can drop in value just as fast as they climb. If you latch onto a red hot subpenny stock, you would be wise to keep an itchy trigger finger and avoid gluttonous gains. Once a subpenny stock turns sour, it usually drops quickly as people try to bail from the stock like rats fleeing a sinking ship.

6

MICROCAP MESSAGE BOARDS

Unlike large and mid cap stocks, most microcap stocks do not have daily press coverage. While some AMEX and NASDAQ microcaps receive an occasional mention in the press, the majority of microcaps, especially those stocks quoted by the OTCBB or the Pink Sheets, never receive conventional press coverage. About the only time you will ever see a penny stock mentioned in traditional print is when there is a sensational story depicting an elaborate scam bilking investors of their hard earned money. This lack of press coverage created a dilemma for microcap investors…where were they supposed to find information on microcap stocks?

It has been said that necessity is the mother of invention. As such, microcap investors have developed a unique way to communicate news, ideas, tips, and strategies to one another…the online stock message board. With the advent of the internet and online investing, penny stock investors began to utilize message boards to communicate to one another. Online message boards are typically referred to as "the boards" and are often filled with a myriad of unique and interesting characters. Longs, shorts, bashers, hypesters, spammers, naïve newbies, and overbearing bullies can all be found cavorting on stock message boards. Because most online message boards are anonymous forums, people tend to drop their guard and let their alter egos take over. Without a doubt, online message boards are a very interesting and entertaining forum.

Every day, hundreds of thousands of posts are made to online stock message boards. Fact, fiction, speculation, and nonsense are daily fodder at these gatherings. Interpreting stock message board postings can be a tricky business. How do you distinguish rumor from fact? Whom can you trust? Is there a way to discover a legitimate tip amongst all of the garbage? As there is very little regulation concerning the content of message board postings, you would do well to consider most postings as fiction or opinion. One great right in our beloved country is the freedom of speech and, for the most part, this freedom transcends to online message board postings. While most sites have rules against obscenities, racial slurs, and threatening language, they typically allow just about anything to be posted. Simply put, these websites do not have the time or manpower to monitor the incredible volume of daily postings displayed on their pages. Most board services have a link to report posts that violate the "terms of service" agreement and the SEC has a link to report posts containing false or illegal information. Other than that, there is little regulation concerning what can and cannot be posted on an online stock message board. When visiting an online stock message board, a simple rule of thumb to abide is "Reader beware."

Over the years, a number of studies have been conducted to assess the nature and influence of online stock message boards. With the sheer volume of daily postings, many have wondered how these sites affect the world of investing. For the most part, studies suggest that online stock message boards are dominated by "unsophisticated" investors. This statement may be somewhat biased due to the fact that many experts frown upon investments in penny stocks. As penny stocks tend to dominate most online stock message boards, it is easy to see why the studies classify the majority of posters as "unsophisticated". Another influence of penny stocks on the findings of these studies has to do with the types of stocks most frequently associated with online message boards. Studies show that heavily trafficked online message boards are associated with non-dividend paying stocks that have high trading volume and extreme volatility. Again, these are characteristics of most penny stocks. Concerning the actions of posters on stock message boards, research has unearthed some interesting findings. First of all, it has been determined that a very small number of posters generate a majority of board messages. Most seasoned penny stock investors did not need a study to confirm this. I have been on boards where I know for a fact that approximately 75% of the first 1000 posts were generated by no more than 3 people. Another painfully obvious finding of these studies is that many posters possess multiple aliases. Well, of course they do! I personally have about six different aliases that I use on the bull boards. Why the need for multiple aliases you ask? You will find out as this chapter unfolds. An interesting finding of these studies does confirm a nagging suspicion of many microcap investors. It has been determined that during periods of accelerated shorting activity, the number of message board postings increases dramatically. With this dubious increase in postings, it has also been noted that many newly created aliases suddenly appear and that many of these aliases post in a collusionary fashion. Most board veterans refer to these posters as "bashers".

If you have ever frequented an online stock message board, you have no doubt run into the ubiquitous basher. With a sharp tongue and a nasty disposition, the basher stands at the ready to discredit a stock in hopes of driving its price down. What is it that motivates these posters to try to make others lose on their investment? The answer is simple…bashers usually stand to make money by causing others to lose their money. "How so", you ask? There are two ways in which a basher can make money by driving the price of stock south. The first is a simple short sale. The basher or his/her associated firm sells a stock short and attempts to tank the stock in an effort to cover at a significantly reduced price. A second way for the basher to make money is by driving the price of a stock down so that he/she or their associated firm may acquire the security at a discount. Fortunately for bashers, it is much easier to scare someone into selling a stock than it is to convince someone to buy one.

There are many ways to bash a stock and there are many different people that attempt to do so. While there are individual investors that are bashers, the best bashers tend to be "hired hands". Yes, believe it or not, there are people that get paid to post negative sentiments on stock message boards. As long as they do not post outright falsehoods or anything of a slanderous nature, these posters are well within their legal rights to expound their antagonistic opinions. It is very easy to identify an amateur basher from someone that actually knows what they are doing. Most amateur bashers post inane drivel such as "SELL THIS DOG NOW!" or "XYZ IS GOING TO TANK!" Oftentimes, amateur bashers will resort to name calling or engage in personal attacks when bombarding a board with their incessant posts. Thankfully, most online message board websites offer an "ignore" feature to filter out posts from these individuals. While it is often easy to spot an amateur basher, an experienced basher is much more elusive. The mark of a good basher is someone that can create negative sentiment on a board without appearing as an outright basher. A tactful basher will never come right out and bash a stock with his initial postings. He will often present himself as a valuable board resource, posting interesting and intriguing information about the stock he plans to eventually trash. As he gains the board's trust and establishes himself as a respected member of the community, people, especially naïve newbies, begin to pay attention to what he has to say. When the basher reaches this point, he will begin to create negative sentiment by expressing concerns about legitimate issues affecting the company. The basher may point out insider sales or a decline in profitability. Even if all is going well for a corporation, a good basher can create doubt by expressing concerns about the future viability of a company's business plan or technology. Because this information is coming from a "trusted source", some investors will heed the basher's warning and sell their shares. Fear tends to be contagious and a good basher combined with a tentative board and a declining stock can create a panic. While such a situation will not affect a high volume large or mid cap stock, a microcap stock with trading volume of less than 100,000 shares can easily succumb to such tactics.

While making money is the ultimate objective of most bashers, a third reason for the actions of bashers is a need to be a thorn in the side of investors. Simply put, some people enjoy creating misery and woe for others. The fact that online stock message boards are an anonymous forum only fuels this opportunity. I must admit that even I have an alias which I use to harass particular boards. It's funny, you can spend a lot of time and effort in creating an informative, well researched post that will often inspire little interest on a message board. On the other hand, if you post something negative about a stock, that one meaningless post will often generate a number of responses. These reactionary postings often originate from diehard longs who think their stock is the best thing since sliced bread. Sometimes, just for fun, I will pepper a board with a few negative posts just to spark the ire of these individuals. It's amazing how long some of these guys spend on a message board. You can post something at 2:30am on a

Sunday night and someone will be on the board to respond to your post. Like the studies show, the most frequent posters tend to spend an inordinate amount of their free time monitoring the bull boards.

Just as the basher seems to be a regular fixture on most message boards, the diehard long and the incessant hypester are often his counterparts. Without fail, you can find these posters on the same board nearly every single day. The diehard long has often been on the board for months or years and is usually there because he bought the stock long ago and has since been sitting on a losing or stagnant investment. Instead of cutting his loses and moving on to greener pastures, the diehard long will hold out hope for an eventual positive return or, at least, a chance to break even on his investment. While I have found most longs to be sensible individuals, some diehard longs seem to think that their stock can do no wrong and they will viciously attack anyone that says otherwise. I have developed a theory as to why the diehard long acts in this fashion. Simply put, the diehard long has often put all of his eggs in one basket. That one stock comprises the bulk of his investment portfolio and he is betting his future on the ascension of said stock. In effect, if you meddle with his one beloved stock, you are meddling with his hopes and dreams. When you run into one of these individuals, check his posting history. More often than not, you will find that nearly all of his postings are limited to the message board of a single stock. Additionally, you will most likely find that this guy is one of the posters that generates a majority of the messages on the board. I recently observed a particularly active poster that generated a huge amount of message board traffic. In one day alone, this person posted 145 messages to the same board. In one month, his total approached 1,000 posts! If you factor in the spam that this guy spread to other boards, this total nearly doubled.

Like the diehard long and the ubiquitous basher, the incessant hypester is a regular fixture on the message boards. While many consider the basher to be a pesky annoyance, the hypester can be just as irritating. The hypester often generates a huge number of posts and most of them tend to be pure trash, completely lacking in truthfulness or substance. Pie-in-the-sky projections and baseless speculations are often the contents of a hypester's post. One glaring difference between a hypester and a basher is the locale of their postings. While a basher tends to focus his efforts on a single message board, the hypester will often spam his message to many boards in an effort to increase visibility for his stock. The reasoning of the hypester is logical enough: spread the word to as many people as possible and hopefully someone will bite. To tell the truth, I have acquired a few investments via the messages of a spamming hypester. If you find a hypester post intriguing, you would be wise to treat the post with a grain of salt and to use it as a base to begin your due diligence. More often than not, you will find the hypester has combined an element of truth with a generous helping of wishful speculation.

The basher, the long, the hypester…quite a cast of characters, eh? In the grand scheme of things, what effect do these guys have on the stocks that they try to influence? Studies have shown that the message boards have little effect on heavily traded stocks. Most large and midcap stocks have daily dollar trading volumes that negate the effects of individual investors as these stocks tend to be dominated by institutional investors. In effect, this fact eliminates most NYSE and NASDAQ stocks from the influence of the bull boards. Microcaps, on the other hand, are a different story. Because many of these stocks tend to be associated with light daily dollar trading volume, the actions of a few posters have the potential to greatly influence trading activity. I recently saw an example of this with the stock Reliant Home Warranty Corporation (OTCBB: RHWC). Here is the story…

From January to March of 2006, one particular poster had been touting the potential of a stock named LVCP. Some would even go so far as to call this guy a hypester, for he spread the word about LVCP to multiple message boards. Despite his best efforts, few investors paid attention to the posts of this person. With time, these investors later kicked themselves for ignoring this individual. From his initial posts at twenty cents, LVCP would eventually rise to over $8! With the astronomical gains of LVCP, this particular poster garnered quite a following of appreciative investors. Things got to a point to where this poster was treated like Smith Barney…when he spoke, people listened! This was evidenced when the poster in question began to tout the potential of RHWC. As previously mentioned, many investors failed to heed our poster's call of LVCP and they missed out on enormous profits. They did not intend to make the same mistake twice. Within 24 hours of his initial mention of the stock, RHWC began to rise. Despite the fact that this stock did not even have a message board, this poster's single mention of RHWC sent the stock flying. Over the next week, RHWC traded an average of 300,000 shares per day and nearly doubled in value. Considering that RHWC had been averaging about 50,000 shares per day prior to the plug by our poster, the influence of a message board on the trading activity of a stock is readily apparent.

7

MICROCAP SHORT SALES

According to many investors, short sales are one of the most confusing aspects of microcap stocks. It seems as if the general investing public has no clue as to the rules regarding this matter. To test this theory, I anonymously posted some questions regarding short selling microcap stocks on a few message boards. The responses that I received were quite varied. One respondent confidently informed me that you could not short stocks costing less than $5. Another poster said that it was $4. Many posters flatly stated that OTCBB and Pink Sheet stocks cannot be shorted. My favorite explanation, and this one was definitely the most off-the-wall, was that terrorists were naked short selling US stocks via foreign exchanges in an effort to undermine the US economy! Obviously, there is some definite confusion regarding microcap short selling amongst layman investors. To clear up this confusion, let's take a look at short selling microcap stocks.

As you all know, I am not an investment professional. I am neither a securities broker/dealer, market maker nor do I work for any type of investment firm. Like you, I am an individual investor. As such, I too had questions regarding the short selling of microcap securities, specifically OTCBB and Pink Sheet stocks. To find some answers, I decided to go straight to the source. First, I called the NASD. Since, according to the SEC, the NASD oversees the OTCBB, I felt that this would be the logical place to start. I called the NASD and a secretary transferred me to the proper department. Of course, no one was available to take my call, so I left a voice-mail. To my surprise, someone from the NASD actually called me back by the end of the day. Unfortunately, this particular NASD representative must have been a summer intern because she had no idea what I was talking about. Each time I asked a question, I could hear her typing on the computer to find the answer on the NASD website. As expected, this person could not answer any of my questions and with each query I was informed to visit the NASD website. I politely informed the rep that I had already visited the NASD website and that I had additional questions. Eventually, the rep gave up and told me to call the SEC. Wow, that was a lot of help! By sheer coincidence, I just happen to live just a few short miles from the NASD's Rockville, Maryland office. I thought that if I went to the NASD in person, maybe someone could provide me with some answers. I drove down to the NASD offices and requested to speak to someone regarding the short selling of OTCBB securities. An NASD employee asked if I was part of an NASD member firm. Upon hearing my negative answer, the NASD employee told me that since I was not a member of an NASD firm, no one could help me. They did, however, provide me with a phone number to an NASD department that could answer all of my questions. Guess what the phone number was? It was the number to the summer intern!

Well, my NASD experience was a bust so I took the summer intern's advice and called upon the SEC for help. I gave the SEC a buzz and reached the ubiquitous secretary. Like the NASD secretary, the SEC secretary thanked me for calling and transferred my call to the "correct" department. The "correct" department must be a secret code word for voice mail because that is exactly what I got. As instructed by the soothing computer generated voice, I left my message with a number where I could be reached. Guess what....I am still waiting for that SEC phone call. I guess they don't have time to talk to the common man. I thought about heading down to D.C. and paying the SEC a personal visit, but I figured it would be a fruitless endeavor and, besides, the Metro trip costs five bucks. Thanks for the help guys! Even if I was able to talk to someone down at the SEC, I am sure that I would have been given the standard company line of "Go check the website."

I'll tell you what, just for grins, let's check out the SEC and NASD websites to see if they can answer the mysterious questions about short selling microcap securities. First up is the SEC website. Some documents on the SEC website are actually fairly helpful. Regarding short sales, the SEC website notes that a short sale occurs when an investor sells a stock that he or she does not own. To do so, the seller borrows shares from their broker and sells them at the current bid. The seller must then cover their short position at a later date by purchasing shares of the short sold stock. Logically, the short seller anticipates that the price of the stock in question will decline and that they will be able to purchase to cover their short position at a lower price.

The SEC has long recognized that unregulated short selling can undercut the price of a stock and lead to manipulative trading strategies such as "bear raids." In such situations, a concerted effort is made to short a stock with the intent of creating significant downward momentum to negatively affect market sentiment towards the security. As this occurs, many investors will have stop-loss orders triggered leading to a further decline and others will eventually capitulate with panic selling. To deter such beguiling practices, the SEC adopted rules and regulations that attempt to control short selling. SEC Rule 10a-1 of the Securities Exchange Act of 1934 introduced provisions commonly referred to as "tick tests" in an effort to thwart short selling in a declining market. With such tests, stocks may only be sold short on a "plus tick" or on a "zero plus tick." A plus tick occurs when the price of a short sale executes at a price higher than the most immediate preceding sale while a zero plus tick occurs when the price of a short sale executes at a price equal to the most immediate preceding sale so long as that price was higher the next immediate preceding sale. While this SEC rule applied to most exchange listed securities, they did not apply to NASDAQ listed stocks. The NASD remedied this situation in 1994 with the implementation of Rule 3350, commonly referred to as the "bid test". Similar to SEC Rule 10a-1, NASD Rule 3350 prohibited short sales in NASDAQ securities at prices equal to or lower than the current best bid when that bid was lower than the most immediate best bid price. In essence, both the bid and tick tests prevent short sales during declining market conditions. Unfortunately, these rules do not apply to OTCBB or Pink Sheet stocks.

Allright! We are making some definite progress in our quest to learn about short selling microcap stocks. To be quite honest, I must admit that the SEC website was helpful. For this I say, "Kudos to you SEC!" Now let's see what we can find on the NASD website. I am feeling pretty confident with this one. The NASD homepage boldly states, "We believe that the most potent form of investor protection is investor education." Well that sounds pretty good. Let's see if the NASD can educate us. I visit the investor information page and click the frequently asked questions link. This link says that I can get answers to commonly asked questions, so let's see if "short selling microcaps" is one of them. The top ten most commonly asked questions pop up and eight of the ten questions deal with information for professional brokers. No information on short selling here. Let's use the search tool and see what happens. I do a little bit of sleuthing and I come up with *NASD Notice to Members 06-28-June 2006: SEC Approves New Rule 3210 Applying Short Sale Delivery Requirements to Non-Reporting OTC Equity Securities; Effective Date July 3, 2006*. Alrighty then! Now we are talking. Let's see what this update has to say:

> "On April 4, 2006, the Securities and Exchange Commission (SEC) approved new Rule 3210, Short Sale Delivery Requirements, which applies short sale delivery requirements to those equity securities not otherwise covered by the delivery requirements of Regulation SHO, namely non-reporting OTC equity securities.[1] Rule 3210, among other things, requires participants of registered clearing agencies to take action on failures to deliver that exist for 13 consecutive settlement days in certain non-reporting securities. In addition, if the fail to deliver position is not closed out in the requisite time period, a participant of a registered clearing agency or any broker-dealer for which it clears transactions is prohibited from effecting further short sales in the particular specified security without borrowing, or entering into a bona-fide arrangement to borrow, the security until the fail to deliver position is closed out."

Okay, now we are getting somewhere. Rule 3210 essentially applies the delivery requirements of Regulation SHO to OTCBB and Pink Sheet stocks. So, what in the heck is Regulation SHO? Back to the NASD search feature. Ah yes, here we go, Regulation SHO. Wow, my query returned a paltry 3,642 documents. That should be easy to navigate! A little more searching and I find some information on Regulation SHO.

> "Regulation SHO, among other things, imposes uniform delivery requirements on broker-dealers for certain securities that have a substantial level of failures to deliver at a registered clearing agency, referred to as "threshold securities." Regulation SHO requires broker-dealers that are participants of a registered clearing agency (clearing agency participants) to take action to "close-out" failure-to-deliver positions in threshold securities that have persisted for 13 consecutive settlement days by purchasing securities of like kind and quantity."

With the implementation of Regulation SHO, the SEC has consolidated locate and close-out rules related to short selling. Rule 203 of Regulation SHO requires broker-dealers executing a short sale to locate securities to borrow before selling and requires broker-dealers to maintain documentation of their compliance with this rule. Additionally, Rule 203 of Regulation SHO also imposes delivery requirements on broker-dealers for securities in which a substantial number of failures to deliver have occurred. This rule requires brokers to close out positions for which they are responsible in securities designated as "threshold securities" after ten consecutive days. If a clearing broker has a fail to deliver position for thirteen consecutive settlement days, said broker is prohibited from executing short sales until the locate requirement is fulfilled.

According to the SEC, "Regulation SHO provides a new regulatory framework governing the short selling of securities. Regulation SHO is designed, in part, to fulfill several objectives, including (1) establish uniform locate and delivery requirements in order to address problems associated with failures to deliver, including potentially abusive "naked" short selling (*i.e.*, selling short without having borrowed the securities to make delivery); (2) create uniform marking requirements for sales of all equity securities; and (3) establish a procedure to temporarily suspend

Commission and SRO short sale price tests in order to evaluate the overall effectiveness and necessity of such restrictions." Blah, blah, blah. The documents regarding Regulation SHO go on for days on end. As an added bonus, they are peppered with language only a lawyer could love.

In my quest to dig up information on Rule 3210 and Regulation SHO, I found this interesting tidbit of information. Reports on the web regarding a recent meeting of the Securities Industries Association (SIA) noted that the SIA was successful in its bid to significantly weaken Regulation SHO. It was reported that the SIA fought tooth and nail to oppose language in the regulation that would have required its members to locate and contractually borrow a security prior to executing a short sale. Instead, the language of Rule 203(b) "creates a uniform Commission rule requiring a broker-dealer, prior to effecting a short sale in any equity security, to "locate" securities available for borrowing." The language of the rule also states that a broker/dealer can execute a short sale so long as they have "reasonable grounds to believe that the security can be borrowed so that it can be delivered on the date delivery is due." I don't know about you, but that type of language sounds like it favors the investment professionals and reduces protection for the common man.

A few paragraphs ago I mentioned a "threshold security." What in the heck is a threshold security? Regulation SHO Rule 2003(c)(6) defines a "threshold security" as any equity security of any issuer that is registered under Section 12 of the Exchange Act, or that is required to file reports under Section 15(d) of the Exchange Act (commonly referred to as reporting securities), where, for five consecutive settlement days: There are aggregate fails to deliver at a registered clearing agency of 10,000 shares or more per security, the level of fails is equal to at least one-half of one percent of the issuer's total shares outstanding, and the

security is included on a list published by a self-regulatory organization (SRO). The NASDAQ publishes a Regulation SHO Threshold Security List for NASDAQ-listed issues, OTCBB issues, and Other-OTC issues on each settlement day prior to midnight, Eastern Time. Additionally, in support of NASD Rule 3210, the NASDAQ, as the NASD's service provider, will expand the Regulation SHO Threshold Securities List to include non-reporting OTC equity securities (Pink Sheet stocks) effective July 11, 2006. The list can be viewed at the following link: http://www.nasdaqtrader.com/aspx/regsho.aspx
On June 14, 2006 there were 166 stocks on the Threshold Securities List. As expected, many of the stocks on this list were OTCBB securities, but there were a surprisingly high number of NASDAQ securities as well.

One final item to note on the NASD website regarding the short selling of microcap securities is *NASD Notice to Members 06-14-April 2006: SEC Approves Amendments to the Short Interest Reporting Requirements; Effective Date July 3, 2006*. According to this notice, the SEC has approved amendments to Rule 3360 expanding short interest reporting requirements to OTC equity securities. Prior to this amendment, Rule 3360(a) required NASD members to maintain a record of total short positions in all customer and proprietary firm accounts in only NASDAQ securities and required members to report such data to the NASD on a monthly basis. Reporting for OTC securities was not required. For the purpose of this rule, OTC equity securities are defined as any equity security that is not listed on the NASDAQ or a national securities exchange. As the OTCBB and Pink Sheets are technically not exchanges, Rule 3360 previously did not apply to these stocks. Now, with the approval of the amendment to Rule 3360, NASD member firms will be required to report their short positions for OTCBB and Pink Sheet stocks.

Well, I guess the NASD summer intern was correct. You can find information regarding short selling microcaps on the NASD and SEC websites, but I hope you have a lot of patience and a penchant for legalese. Although I never found a *direct answer* to my questions, it is apparent that shorting of microcaps including OTCBB and Pink Sheet stocks is definitely allowed. While this is true for the investing professional, most of us common folk are prohibited from shorting these stocks via restrictions from our brokerage firms on marginable trades. Federal Reserve Regulation T requires investors to utilize margin accounts to post collateral for short sales. Most brokerage firms use this regulation to prevent investors from shorting most microcaps. E-Trade, for example, reports that stocks under $2 are not marginable. Schwabb reports that marginable stocks must be traded on a major exchange and cost $3 or more. Scottrade reports that stocks costing less than $5 are not shortable. In effect, by imposing regulations on marginable accounts via minimum pricing and exchange membership requirements, most brokerage firms have indirectly prohibited the common man from shorting the majority of microcap stocks. Each brokerage firm has their own rules and regulations regarding the short selling of securities, so be sure to check with your broker for specifics.

Naked Short Sales

Now that we have discussed short selling microcap stocks, let's turn our attention to a subject that is even more mysterious and controversial…naked short selling. Nearly every penny stock investor has heard about naked shorting. In fact, if a penny stock begins to tank, you will undoubtedly see someone posting that the stock is being killed by naked shorting. Just what exactly is naked shorting? To find out, let's check back with our friends at the

NASD. During my conversation with the alleged summer intern, I posed a question about naked shorting. Once again, the rep could not answer my question. She kept babbling on about short selling rules (as she read them off of her computer screen), but could not answer any of my questions about naked shorting. To be honest, I don't think she knew what naked short selling was! Clueless…simply clueless. I gave up that line of questioning and decided to check the NASD website. Utilization of the search feature returned 1,704 documents when the words "naked shorting" were queried. Of course, none of the documents I examined specifically dealt with naked shorting directly and if they did mention anything about it, the information was buried deep within the confines of the document. I did find an NASD document stating "NASD rules restrict *naked* short sales, that is selling a stock short without ensuring that the stock can be borrowed or otherwise provided for by settlement date, also known as an affirmative determination." For all intensive purposes, the NASD provided me with few answers for my research on naked shorting. Once again, thanks for the help guys.

Since my NASD search proved relatively fruitless, I turned to the SEC for assistance. As you might have guessed, my attempts to talk with an actual human being associated with the SEC were nonproductive. I, therefore, attempted to utilize the SEC website. By making use of the search feature on the SEC website, my query for naked shorting returned 1,100 documents regarding naked shorting. Unlike the NASD website, however, the SEC website ranked these documents in order of relevance and some of the documents were easy to read and went right to the point. My review of the documents on the SEC website noted that naked short selling distorts market pricing by creating artificial supply/demand imbalances that benefit the manipulator. Well, everyone knows that. What we need is more specific information regarding naked shorting. By digging a little deeper, the SEC website noted that naked short sellers have the ability to destabilize the market for a stock due to the lack of enforceable restrictions requiring the actual borrowing of securities prior to a executing a short sale. As such, the inability to borrow said securities creates a "fail-to-deliver" situation. As shares are naked shorted and, therefore, are not actually borrowed, the potential exists for the number of fails in a stock to actually outnumber the public float for the stock. This point is easily demonstrated by the very famous story of Robert Simpson. In early 2005, Mr. Simpson filed documents with the SEC concerning his purchase of 100% of the issued and outstanding stock for the Global Links Corporation. As legend has it, Mr. Simpson stuck all of his Global Links stock in his sock drawer for safe keeping. Despite the fact that Mr. Simpson had every share of this company safely nestled next to his tidy whities, this OTCBB stock still somehow managed to trade nearly 60 million shares in the two days following his SEC filing! Can this really happen? You bet it can!

Tom Ronk, founder of BUYINS.Net, a California based internet firm that researches and reports on companies that are targets of abusive or naked short selling practices, has said that nearly 20% of publicly traded companies have been naked shorted between 2005-mid 2006. According to Mr. Ronk, "BUYINS.Net has built a proprietary database that uses list feeds to generate detailed and useful information to combat the naked short selling problem." Additionally, Ronk noted that, "…actual trade by trade data is available to the public that shows the volume, price, and average value of short sales in stocks that have been shorted and naked shorted." According to the website, BUYINS.net utilizes its massive database of nearly 800 million short sale transactions dating back to January of 2005 to calculate "Squeeze Trigger Prices" to alert investors to the exact price point when a short squeeze can start. The Squeeze Trigger database collects individual short trade data on over 7,000 NYSE, NASDAQ, and

AMEX stocks as well as general short trade data on nearly 8,000 OTCBB and Pink Sheet stocks. BUYINS.net provides this service for a very nominal fee. To date, BUYINS.net is one of the few services available to investors for combating abusive short selling and naked short selling practices. This website is definitely worth a look. Check it out at http://www.buyins.net

With such a potentially enormous problem, you would think that the mainstream press would focus more attention on naked shorting. One of the biggest whistleblowers regarding naked shorting has been Dr. Patrick Byrne, CEO of Overstock.com. According to his posts on the Overstock.com message board, Dr. Byrne equates naked shorting to counterfeiting shares. Because the naked short seller does not actually borrow the shares that he is selling, these shares are, in essence, simply made up. As such, there is no limit to how many bogus shares that hedge funds can create. Dr. Byrne presents multiple scenarios as to how naked shorting can occur in our "regulated" U.S. market place. One theory essentially states that a "Good-ole-boy" network exists on Wall Street whereby the Depository Trust and Clearing Corporation (DTCC, the agency that keeps electronic records of who owns which stock at which brokerages, and settles the trading of stocks) and various brokers look the other way for favored clients. A second explanation insinuates that hedge funds will list a U.S. stock on a foreign exchange without the permission or knowledge of the parent company and will utilize this listing to naked short the stock in question. When contacted by the DTCC to locate and deliver the shorted shares, the fund will reference the foreign exchange in an effort to buy time and allow their naked short position to continue. While this sounds quite fantastic, many companies have indeed found their stock to be listed on foreign exchanges without their knowledge. In fact, Dr. Byrne noted that in late 2004, Overstock.com was listed on five German exchanges and one in Australia. None of these listings were ever requested by the company.

When I think about naked short selling, I wonder why it takes the CEO of a large company to bring this matter to the attention of the investing public. The media reports on every detail of a celebrity's life and runs stories on every minor political scandal, yet they rarely mention a problem that is costing honest investors billions of dollars. I wonder why a private company such as BUYINS.net can research and create lists of naked shorted stocks while regulatory agencies such as the SEC and NASD, which are supposed to protect investors, cannot or will not do the same. Others, it seems, are beginning to wonder the same thing. A recent online survey of nearly 2,500 U.S. adults found that 38% of respondents would be more likely to vote for a congressional candidate that would address the issue of naked shorting. Congress, it seems, is starting to get the message. In a 2005 hearing of the Senate Banking Committee, Utah Senator Robert Bennett questioned former SEC Chairman William Donaldson about the potential shortcomings of Regulation SHO by noting ways that collusive brokers could get around the regulation. Perhaps the issue of naked shorting will receive more attention during upcoming elections.

Simply put, naked shorting is an illegal practice that may be costing investors billions of dollars. Some reports have estimated that the extent of naked shorting on Wall Street could be up to 100 times greater than the alleged $10.5 billion short position of the disgraced financial firm Refco. While this practice appears to affect stocks of all sizes, microcap stocks tend to be commonly victimized as many are fairly illiquid and make easy targets for unscrupulous naked short sellers. Though the SEC and NASD have recently announced new regulations to improve the environment of short sales, it is obvious that the issue of naked short selling still has much to be addressed.

8

CONTEMPORARY MICROCAP TRADING STRATEGIES

For the uninitiated, buying and selling penny stocks can be a frustrating and costly endeavor. Over the years, I have seen far too many investors stumble into the pitfalls of penny stock investing (myself included). That was the impetus for the creation of my first book *Penny Stocks: The Next American Gold Rush*. If you are an advanced or experienced microcap investor you may want to skip this chapter as it is a basic review intended to indoctrinate those new to penny stock investing.

If you are new to penny stock or microcap investing, you need to understand that trading these stocks can be much different than what you are used to on the larger exchanges. The key item to consider here is where your stock is traded. Trading on the NASDAQ and AMEX is basically similar to what you are used to with normal stocks. One key difference between NASDAQ or AMEX penny stocks and their more expensive brethren is that most brokerage firms will not allow margin activity on stocks that sell for less than five dollars. Other than that, trading these stocks on said exchanges is virtually the same as what you are used to.

When you begin trading penny stocks on the OTCBB or Pink Sheets, you have entered a different world of investing. If you fail to comprehend this, you are destined to lose money and gain frustration as you trip and fall on the little nuances that are unique to trading on these markets.

As mentioned other times in this text, the first rule of trading on the OTCBB or Pink Sheets is to NEVER EVER PLACE A MARKET ORDER! The open market order is the most common mistake that I see inexperienced investors make when trading penny stocks. If you learn one thing from this book, this is what you should remember. Unlike the larger exchanges which are required to execute your order in a timely manner, transaction executions on the OTCBB and Pinks are at the discretion of the market makers. In other words, there is no guarantee that your order will be filled at the current market price if you place a market order. An open market order tells the market makers that you are willing to pay the market price for a stock. On the larger exchanges where transactions occur virtually instantaneously, you usually get your stock for the listed price when you click the buy button. On the OTCBB and Pinks, this may not be the case. With an open market order, there is a chance that the market makers will raise the asking price of a stock prior to filling the buy order. Hey, don't blame the market makers. You said that you were willing to pay the going rate for the stock and there is no rule that says they have to fill your order immediately.

When trying to buy an OTCBB or Pink Sheet stock, you must be sure that you place a limit buy order. In the event that you forget this little piece of advice, some brokerage firms *require* that you place a limit order for buy or sell orders. This will protect you from the dangers of the open market order. While the limit buy order will protect you from fluctuations in the asking price, the market makers still have a few tricks up their sleeve for you. With a limit buy order, you are telling the market makers that you would like to buy a stock, but that you are only willing to pay a certain price or less for said stock. To counter your offer, the market makers may increase the asking price without filling your order in an effort to make you raise your limit price. When the ask increases, some investors get excited and think that they must increase their limit order to avoid missing a run. Don't fall for this trap.

When placing an order to buy a stock, I will often set my limit either at the bid or at a price somewhere between the bid and the ask. If the order is for an OTCBB or Pink Sheet stock, the market makers usually won't fill such an order in a timely fashion. Instead of filling the order, the market makers will often bump up the ask. When this occurs, I am generally content to let my order sit. Unless the market is moving quickly and I really want a piece of the stock, I will not take the market makers' bait. Sometimes my order will stay open for hours while other times it will not fill at all. In many cases, I have found that the market makers tend to fill open orders such as these near the end of the trading day. My philosophy is not to chase the ask if I can avoid it. I really despise it when the market makers try this tactic. Seriously, we are here to buy and sell stocks, not play games! Unfortunately, because the market makers have enormous power on the OTCBB and Pink Sheets, you must learn to play their games if you want to be successful. With a slowly moving stock, you can challenge the market makers to a certain degree. However, doing the same on a stock with heavy volume may not be possible. I have traded many high volume stocks where I have had to take the market makers' bait and raise my limit buy in order to get a position in the stock. The market was hot and the stock was moving quickly. If I did not raise my limit price, my order would have never been filled. You must decide how high you are willing to go when chasing the ask. With a fast moving stock, many investors will chase the ask too high, raising their limit orders multiple times in the process. Greed is what drives this process as investors don't want to miss the run. If the price is moving north rapidly, investors want in. Sometimes they want it so badly that they don't realize they are being taken for a ride.

Now that we have talked about buying OTCBB and Pink Sheet stocks, let's turn our attention to selling these stocks. Like a market buy order, the market sell order can lead to trouble. If you indicate that you are willing to sell at the market rate, the market makers may quickly drop the bid prior to filling your order. Placing such a frivolous order may not only cause problems for you, it may also cause problems for everyone else as well. Let me tell you a little story about a crazy day of trading for one particular pink sheet stock. The stock in question is International Power Group (Pink Sheets: IPWG). Now, as you will soon see, I love to trade this stock. You can read more about IPWG in the alternative energy section of the chapter titled *Sectors Poised for Profit*.

Let me start this story off by saying that I am speculating about what happened on this particular day. No one can ever be sure of exactly what happens during a trading day. It's not like you can gather all of the stock's market makers in a single room and quiz them on the day's activities. So, let us begin our story. One fine October day, IPWG was flying high, enjoying a two week run of uninterrupted gains. The morning was progressing just like every other morning of the previous two weeks as new fifty two week highs were being set left and right. Then, like a heavy black cloud ruining a beautiful day, a thoughtless investor placed a market sell order. My guess is that this guy was an uninformed newbie who was ready to cash in on the large gains produced by the recent two week run. Around noon, the market sell order hit the wire and the market makers quickly dropped the bid in an effort to acquire this guy's shares at dirt cheap prices. This transaction led to an unfortunate series of events that cost investors big bucks. As the bid quickly fell to fill the open market order, open stop-loss orders were triggered and this resulted in additional selling. This sales wave created a small panic among investors and weak hands began to bail out of their positions. When the smoke had cleared at the end of the trading day, the once mighty stock that was setting new fifty two week highs earlier in the day had declined by nearly 50%.(see figure 11) Can you believe that? A 50% drop in price on a day with no negative news or SEC filing activity. Such a precipitous drop would be unheard of on the larger exchanges, but it is not unusual for a Pink Sheet stock.

I must say that I was partly to blame for the activity on that particular day. I was one of the investors that had an open stop-loss order. Unless you have the luxury of watching your stocks all day long, it is highly advisable to place a stop-loss order on your microcap investments. A stop-loss order will protect you from sudden drops in the price of a stock. But you must be careful when placing a stop-loss order. If you set the stop-loss order at a value that is too close to the current price of the stock, there is a good chance that the stock's normal intraday trading activity will trigger your open order and cause the sale of your stock. By the time that my stop-loss order filled, I ended up with a nice profit on the sale of my stock. Before I took the time to count my money, I watched the rest of the day's activity and feverishly determined a re-entry price to get back into the stock. I was banking on the fact that this unsubstantiated price reduction would quickly be followed by a rebound. I placed a limit buy order at a price that was slightly lower than what the market makers were willing to fill. On the following morning, I had to fiddle with my purchase price, but I eventually reacquired my shares for a significant discount. As I had expected, the day after the tanking was indeed a rebound day as the stock finished up 33% by the close. These two crazy days underscore the extreme volatility of OTCBB and Pink Sheet stocks. Prices move quickly on these markets and if you are not paying attention, you could be in for a big surprise.

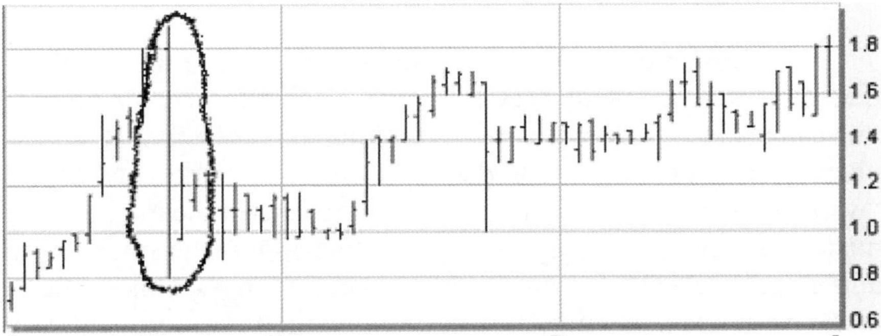

Figure 11: Highlight of October 2005 trading day in which IPWG stock experienced extreme volatility. IPWG opened the trading day at $1.80 and hit an intraday high of $1.90 setting a new 52 week high. As the day progressed the stock's price dropped dramatically hitting an intraday low of $0.80. That is nearly a 60% change in value for a single day! The stock closed for the day at $0.90. Note the rebound that occurred on the following day. The stock gapped up nearly 10% at the open and finished with a gain of over 30% for the day. These two days presented an excellent trading opportunity! A day like this would never happen on the larger markets. Notice that the stock recovered very nicely over the next few months. Had you taken advantage of the activity on this particular October day, you could have sold for a profit and used your gains to reacquire the stock with a larger position at reduced prices. Also note that the stock had a second volatile day in November.

Now, you must be wondering if this scenario is really possible. Can a few sell orders trigger such a sell-off? Well, first of all, let me clarify things by saying that an event like this is not likely to occur on the larger exchanges. An event such as this can only occur with thinly traded stocks, typical of many securities that are found on the OTCBB and Pink Sheets. Stocks with heavy daily volume have the ability to absorb such orders without them having much effect on trading activity. Thinly traded stocks however, may go an entire day with only a few trades. When a stock has minimal trading activity, a few sell orders can do a lot of damage!

Thinly traded stocks have little volume, hence the “thinly traded” adjective. Many OTCBB stocks fit this description and this can lead to a few problems. One common problem that plagues investors of thinly traded stocks is when market makers “walk down” a stock. Walking down occurs when the market makers slowly decrease a stock’s value by gapping the stock lower at the opening bell over numerous consecutive days. This subtle tactic frustrates many investors into selling their positions which contributes to a further decline in the value of the stock. Another situation resulting from low volume is the increased spread. Actually, this is a debatable point similar to “what came first, the chicken or the egg?” Basically, an increased spread means that there is a great difference between the bid and the asking price for a stock. Often this spread is so wide that it scares off many potential investors. For example, a stock asking twenty cents and bidding fifteen cents has a spread of 25%. If you were to buy this stock, you would immediately take a huge loss if you were to sell. On the larger markets, the bid and ask are usually a penny or two different. No big deal. However, if the stock you are trading only costs a nickel, a one cent difference between the bid and the ask *is* a big deal! Who wants to buy a stock like that? No one does and that is exactly what happens in most cases. You must consider this point carefully when deciding to trade a penny stock. You may feel that you have found the greatest stock in the world, but if it has no volume it is essentially worthless. What good is owning a stock if there is no one around to buy when you want to sell?

As you can see, trading stocks on the OTCBB and Pink Sheets presents its own unique set of challenges. Buying and selling requires caution and finesse. It’s almost like handling a poisonous snake. If you know what you are doing, you can pick up the snake and admire its beauty. If you do things wrong, you are going to get bitten and it is going to hurt badly! While you can treat a snake bite with anti-venom to restore your life, there is no magic potion to put cash back in your wallet should you bumble through an OTCBB or Pink Sheet transaction.

So what if you don't want to handle a snake, but you still want to trade penny stocks? Technically speaking, some consider a penny stock to be anything that trades for five bucks or less. As such, there are a number of AMEX and NASDAQ stocks that easily fit this bill. Before we continue, let me ask you a question. Why limit yourself to penny stocks? Why not consider microcaps? Both offer the ability to acquire shares at relatively cheap prices and both have the potential for large gains. When the markets were flying high five to six years ago, penny stocks made up a large portion of my portfolio. However, after the bursting of the internet bubble, I have shifted to heavier positions in microcap stocks. I still trade OTCBB and Pink Sheet stocks, but they make up a much smaller percentage of my portfolio than they did in the past.

Over the years I have tried many different strategies to find prospective investments. Candle stick analysis, cup & handles, bow-ties, etc…I have tried them all. After dabbling in these various different methodologies, I have come to the realization that I prefer a much simpler approach to finding great investments. In trading microcaps, I have been utilizing a screening strategy that has provided me with some excellent returns. I use a stock screener available on my online broker's website. You can easily do the same. Your stock screener does not need to be fancy and just about any will do. I use a stock screener to locate stocks that fit parameters that I am comfortable with. Upon identification of these stocks, if I like what I see in my due diligence, I will add the stock to my portfolio. In essence, a "microcap mutual fund" is what I have created. In this microcap mutual fund, I tend to have about fifteen to twenty stocks which I constantly monitor and adjust.

To ensure that I get a microcap stock, I set the screener for a maximum share price of twenty dollars and a market cap of $500 million or less. I like stocks that are near their lows, so I set my screener to find stocks that have decreased in value during the past year. Now, this may be contrary to the opinion of many investing experts. Many say that when a stock is going down, it is headed south for a reason. They often advise to wait until the stock has established a sustained upward trend before taking a position. I think that this is sound advice, but it is not what I like to do.

I subscribe to the "Blood in the streets" theory of investing where you pick up shares in stocks when they are at their lowest. These stocks are usually down in the dumps and no one has anything good to say about them. As Warren Buffet once said, "…be greedy when others are fearful!" Well, nothing tends to strike fear in the heart of an investor more than a tanking stock. Blood in the street investing is not for everyone as it can be a very gut wrenching process. To buy a stock when everyone else is selling takes some strong intestinal fortitude. You must also be willing to sacrifice some time. Unless you have a magic crystal ball, there is no telling when the stock in question is going to right its course. As it is impossible to predict the bottom for these stocks, I usually purchase them on a downtrend and they often continue south after I get in. That is okay because I am prepared for this. In fact, I expect it. Many times, if a stock continues to fall, I will do something else that many experts advise against...I will average down. For those of you who don't know what averaging down is, let me give you the down and dirty. To average down, you buy more stock at a lower price. You then divide the total amount of money that you have invested in the stock by the total number of shares that you own to get a new break even price. Now you must realize that I don't do these things by the seat of my pants. I do this because I am confident in the stocks that I have invested in. I gain this confidence by setting my stock screener to find stocks that have sales revenue of at least one million dollars, a positive profit margin, positive earnings growth, positive revenue growth, and a PEG ratio with a maximum of one. I like to use the PEG ratio in lieu of the P/E ratio because the PEG ratio accounts for growth. A PEG ratio of less than one typically indicates that a stock is somewhat undervalued. Finally, I set my screener to look for stocks with daily volume of at least fifty thousand shares. As I have mentioned before, a stock without volume is a dead stock.

After setting the parameters for my stock screener (see figure 12) I then examine each stock individually. I read the company's press releases, read the 10Q's, examine the balance sheet to see how much cash is in the bank versus how much debt is on the books, and finally, I look at how many shares are short. I like it when at least 10% of the float is shorted. I understand that people are shorting the stock because it is down and out. However, when things turn around (if the company fits the parameters that I have set in my screener I have confidence that the company will right the ship) the shorts will eventually cover and this will add fuel to the fire when the stock recovers. Finally, I will visit a few message boards to see if there is any buzz about the stock in question.

Everyone has their own method of investing. What I have just shown you is one of the ways that I am currently investing. With blood in the streets investing, you cannot simply pick up a stock just because it is near its low. There must be other reasons for buying the stock. That is where my stock screener and other identifying factors come in. Sometimes good stocks fall in spite of strong fundamentals. If you can identify such stocks, you can acquire them at a significant discount.

Share price	≤ $20
Market capitalization	≤ $500,000,000
1 year performance	≤ 0%
Revenue	≥ $1,000,000
Profit margin	> 0%
Earnings growth	> 0%
PEG Ratio	< 1
Volume	≥ 100,000 shares

Figure 12: Stock screener parameters
This is an example of the parameters that I set on my stock screener when searching for microcaps. These parameters usually return anywhere from 50 to 100 stocks. I then look at each stock individually for news, pending litigation, cash on hand, debt on the books, shares short, etc.

One of my favorite blood in the streets memories comes from Waste Management Inc. (NYSE: WMI). Back in 1999, WMI was experiencing some difficulties and the stock was tanking hard. From a high of near $60, WMI sunk to lows approaching $12. I actually found this stock by reading an article that mentioned WMI as a blood in the street type of stock. Shortly after reading the article I was driving my car and I just happened to be sitting at a traffic light behind a WMI garbage truck. I remember thinking, "Hey, that truck belongs to the company I just read about." I followed the truck for a while and watched it empty a dumpster in the parking lot of a local convenience store. Prior to reading that article, I never gave trash much thought and I certainly had never heard of WMI. As I continued to drive my car that day, I took note of as many dumpsters as I could. To my amazement, WMI dumpsters were everywhere. They were downright ubiquitous! I never realized that one single company had such a monopoly-like stranglehold on the local waste market. Fundamentally, WMI was a strong company and it was not going to disappear. Within two years of its blood in the streets low point in the year 2000, WMI recovered nicely to yield potential gains approaching 125%. Not bad for an NYSE stock!

Here is an example of a great stock that I found with my stock screener in December of 2004. The stock is aQuantive, Inc. (NASDAQ: AQNT) At the time, the stock was hovering near its fifty two week low and was getting beaten up pretty badly. Using my screening parameters, I liked what I saw in AQNT. News for this stock was satisfactory, cash to debt ratio was acceptable, and message board traffic for AQNT was good. This stock has performed very well over the past year, making gains of over 180%. (see figure 13)

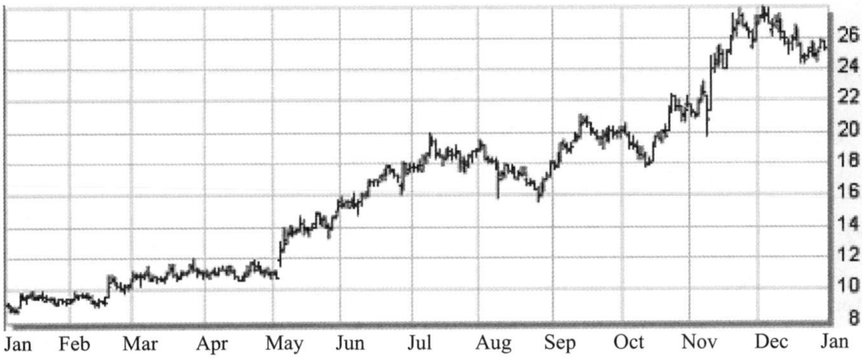

Figure 13: AQNT 1 year chart

Here is an example of a stock that I found with my screener that did not do so well during the past year. The stock is Leadis Technologies, Inc. (NASDAQ: LDIS). When this stock appeared on my screener I liked what I saw. The stock was recovering from a recent downtrend and had some decent numbers. I took a position in the stock in late December of 2004. Wouldn't you know it, within a few weeks of getting into this stock it decides to tank. I cut bait and sold a large portion of my holdings for a loss in January. As time passed, I was kicking myself for not selling my entire position. The stock continued to decline over the next three months before stabilizing in April. When LDIS stabilized and seemed to form a new base, I averaged down and picked up some additional shares. From May to early July, the stock enjoyed a nice recovery but unfortunately tanked again in late July. (see figure 14) I was hoping to get out of this stock with limited losses so I sold my entire position in June in the midst of LDIS's short recovery. I still took a loss on this stock, but it turned out to be less than what it could have been had I held.

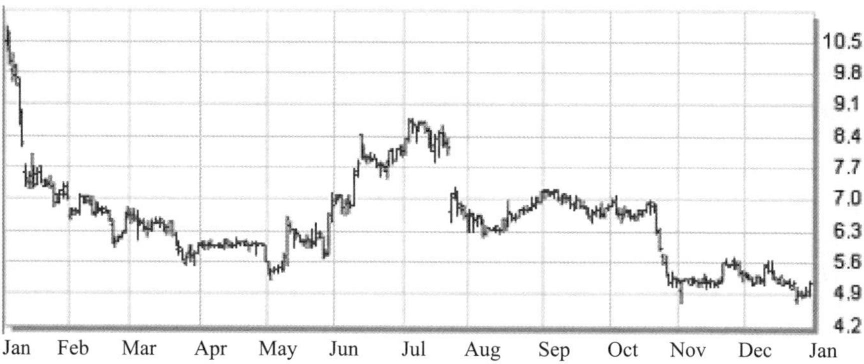

Figure 14: LDIS 1 year chart

I check the stocks in my "microcap mutual fund" once per day, usually at the end of the trading day. Occasionally, I will increase or decrease my holdings in a stock depending on its performance. It is important to keep your portfolio dynamic. If you simply buy a stock and let it sit you are putting yourself at risk in my opinion. I have seen too many cases of investors holding a losing stock way too long in the hope that it will eventually recover. At some point you need to admit that you were wrong on that particular investment and limit your losses. Additionally, by having your money tied up in a losing stock while you wait for its eventual recovery, you will be missing out on many other trading opportunities. On the flip side, you also need to know when you want to take profits on a stock. Just as on the losing side, I have seen far too many investors hold on to a winning stock way too long. By holding too long, I mean that they never take any profits while the stock is up and by the time they do decide to take a profit the stock has significantly receded from its highs. I will typically sell a portion of my holdings in a stock when the security achieves set percentage gain milestones. When the stock takes a dip, I often use my profits to add back to my position. I like to think of this as buying a stock on sale. Everyone loves a good sale. I should know. I spent six hours waiting in lines during this year's day after Thanksgiving sales! When adding to a position, I try not to load up too heavily on one particular stock. No need to put all of your eggs in one basket as they say.

While I like to utilize the stock screener as much as possible to find stocks for my "microcap mutual fund", I also employ other tactics to find gems in the rough. One of these tactics is simply screening the news and reading articles about current events. Upon screening this information, if something catches my eye, I will run a stock screener to see if any stocks fit the story that caught my fancy. Let me give you a few examples.

In November 2004, Ukraine was embroiled in a bitter election dispute that resulted in what is now known as the "Orange Revolution". The incumbent candidate Viktor Yanukovych favored Russia over the West and his economic policies clearly reflected this. The challenger, Viktor Yuschenko, had aligned himself with Western ways and vowed to increase ties with Europe and the United States. I remember thinking to myself, "If this Yuschenko guy wins, I'll bet that he opens Ukraine to Western companies." As Ukraine was still emerging from its post-Soviet economic funk, its economy was still rather underdeveloped. I sensed opportunity! I ran my stock screener for anything related to Ukraine. My search turned up no results so I modified the stock screener to look for anything related to Eastern Europe. I found a small mutual fund, the Morgan Stanley Eastern Europe Fund, Inc. (NYSE: RNE). I checked out the fund and I liked what I saw. It was small with a market cap of $100 million and it had decent volume. I decided that if Yuschenko won the election, I was going to take a position in this particular mutual fund. Justice prevailed in this situation and Yuschenko was declared the winner of the runoff election. The Orange Revolution had worked! The people of Ukraine had pulled off a peaceful coup of a corrupt government and their country would be benefit from their actions. I intended to benefit from their actions as well! Shortly Yuschenko assumed control of Ukraine, my predictions were validated as the small Eastern European mutual fund increased in value by nearly 20%. Over the next few months, news of Ukraine disappeared from the Western press and RNE likewise faded. Over the remainder of the year, however, RNE enjoyed a steady rise and paid a nice fat dividend. Don't be fooled by the chart (figure 15). That dip towards the end of the year reflects the dividend payment.

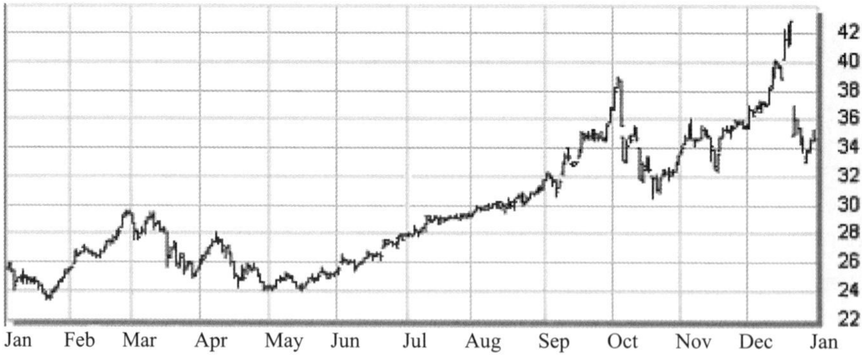

Figure 15: RNE 1 year chart

A second example of a stock I found by simply reading a news story has to do with online gaming in Korea. Wow…these last two picks were pretty worldly. Korea and Ukraine? I would have never guessed that I would be searching for stocks in these two countries. Well, we have to follow the money and if the money is in Korea or Ukraine that is where we are headed! The story I was reading described South Korea's obsession with online gaming. South Korea is one of the most, if not the most, connected country on Earth as far as the internet is concerned. More than half of the population has internet access and cyber cafes can be found on virtually every street corner. I knew that online gaming was catching on here in the states and I once again sensed opportunity knocking. We usually tend to lag a few years behind Japan and Korea as far as high tech toys and gadgets are concerned, so I figured that if online gaming has been hot in Korea, it would soon be just as hot over here. I opened my trusty stock screener and searched for stocks related to online gaming. As luck would have it, I found an online gaming company based in South Korea that trades on the NASDAQ. The stock in question is Webzen, Inc. (NASDAQ: WZEN). When I found this stock it was trading near its fifty two week low. As you can guess, I liked that finding. Webzen had a market cap near $500 million and decent trading volume. I would have liked the company's numbers to have been a little better than what they were, but I was still relatively happy with the stock nonetheless. From its 52 week lows in the latter part of the summer of 2005, WZEN made a striking recovering with gains surpassing 125%. (See figure 16)

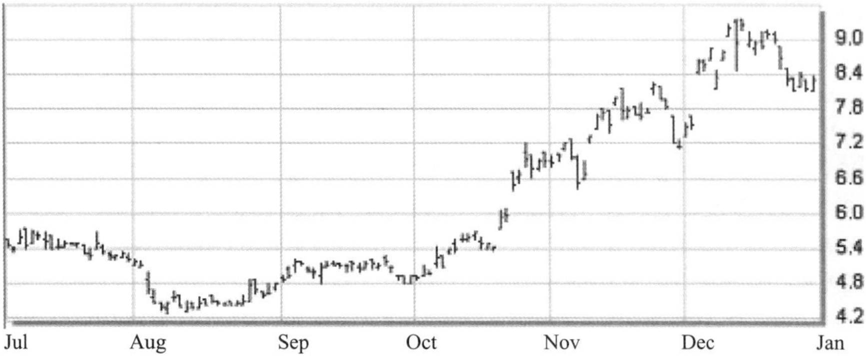

Figure 16: WZEN 1 year chart

One final and much less scientific method I utilize to find potential investments is the "small float" theory. By small float, I am talking about a stock with total tradable shares of ten million or less. In my opinion, the smaller the float the better. Tiny floats lead to extreme volatility and the potential for enormous gains. One problem with small floats is that they are usually associated with stocks that have minimal trading volume. I know, I know…I previously said that a stock without volume is a dead stock. In the case of a tiny float, however, I will make an exception to this rule. Just like me, many seasoned microcap investors love to find stocks with small floats. When someone discovers one of these stocks, word of the find eventually trickles to the online stock message boards. With this exposure, there are usually a number of investors who may take a position in the stock. When this happens, a spike in demand for a stock with a tight float leads to rapid price ascension.

An example of the small float effect was seen with a pink sheet stock called Legend Investment Corporation (Pink Sheets: LVCP). At one time, LVCP was hovering around 60 cents and had minimal trading volume. Less than one year later, LVCP reached highs eclipsing $8! This amazingly fast and robust appreciation in value was accomplished on trading volume averaging approximately 350,000 shares. "How was this possible", you ask? LVCP had a mere 4.68 million shares outstanding and a float of only 364 thousand shares. Talk about a small float! When you consider that this stock was quoted by the Pink Sheets, a float that small is unheard of. Prior to its amazing run, LVCP reeled off a number of positive press releases. These press releases in themselves should have been enough to kick this stock into high gear. The spark for LVCP's explosive movement, however, was the identification of the stock as one with a tiny float. Just before its run, reports of LVCP began popping up on various stock message boards and websites. LVCP was identified as having an extremely small float and the potential for fast gains. For many microcap investors, a small float is like an ultraviolet light to an insect…it is irresistible! Prior to the identification of LVCP as a stock with a small float, its average daily trading volume ranged from 10,000 to 20,000 shares. On a few days, LVCP had no volume at all! After its identification as a small floater, LVCP had immediately had a volume spike approaching 50,000 shares. While this volume is fairly miniscule, the fact that LVCP had a tiny tradable float caused the stock to have an intraday spike of nearly 30%. As LVCP began to issue its positive press releases, its volume improved even more to a daily average of nearly 300,000 shares. For many penny stocks, 300,000 shares could constitute a single transaction, but for LVCP and its tiny float, it provided the impetus for incredible gains. With just a few weeks of "heavy" trading volume, LVCP appreciated nearly 2000%! If you didn't understand my fascination of stocks with small floats, you should now.

I have recently identified a stock with a small float and I am quite excited about its prospects. The stock in question is Fortune Diversified Industries, Inc. (AMEX: FFI). FFI, through its many subsidiaries, is involved in a number of different industries including manufacturing, distribution, professional business solutions, and wireless infrastructure. The company has over 6,000 employees and yearly revenues approaching $140 million. Recent SEC filings show year over year quarterly revenue growth was up 65% and quarterly earnings were up as well. While all of that sounds great, that is not what really interests me. What I really like about FFI is its teeny tiny float of only 825,000 shares! I am really amazed that a stock of this caliber has such a small float. As expected, the average daily trading volume for FFI is extremely small as anywhere from 5,000 to 7,000 shares typically exchange hands on a daily basis. This combination of a low volume and a tiny float is like a powder keg ready to explode. Should this stock ever experience any surge in volume, the limited availability of its tradable shares should create a price eruption. To be quite honest, I see few reasons for FFI's lack of volume. FFI has more than double the revenue of TASR, yet TASR has nearly 550 times the trading volume of FFI and a market capitalization approaching 12 times that of FFI. Eventually, FFI is going to be discovered. A float that small associated with a decent quality stock is not something that you see everyday. When FFI is discovered by the investing public, its share price should rise and that may lead to second benefit for shareholders…stock splits!

9

AVERAGING DOWN

The concept of averaging down is simple enough. You buy a stock at one price, add to your position at a lower price, take the sum total of all of your shares and divide it by the total cash paid for the stock. Many experts abhor averaging down, calling it a habit of amateur investors. The reason for their disdain is the thought that averaging down doubles your position in a losing venture and sets you up for failure. Some say that pride has a part in averaging down, that rather than admit a mistake, investor hubris causes one to dig deeper a hole that may be inescapable.

Contrary to expert opinion, I feel that averaging down is a great tool to have in your bag of tricks. Under the right circumstances, averaging down affords an opportunity for increased profits. While I don't do it on all of my trades, I do average down on quite a few of my positions. As I have mentioned before, I like to buy stocks when they are in a downward trend. Due to the virtual impossibility of timing an initial entry point to coincide with an absolute low, my positions often take a negative turn in their infancy. For some, this would cause panic, but I actually expect this to happen. Now, I know what you are thinking… "if you expect your initial position to *decrease* in value, why not simply wait a little longer before buying the stock?" I will tell you why I do not do this.

While it does not happen often, there are occasions when you are fortunate or lucky enough to buy a stock at its absolute low. I have had this happen twice during the past year with the stocks EVOL and EVCI. As the year of 2004 drew to a close, I was looking for a few stocks to add to my portfolio. One of the stocks highlighted by my stock screener was Evolving Systems (NASDAQ: EVOL). I purchased the stock at around $3.60 and did not expect much to happen with the stock for a while. By sheer luck, the day after making my purchase, the company had some news and the stock took off like a rocket. Trading volume exploded from an average of about one hundred seventy thousand shares to just over five million shares on that particular day. With such feverish trading activity, the price of EVOL stock quickly appreciated to a high of $4.90. This action was much more than I had anticipated and I sold my entire position to lock in a fast profit. Sometimes you get lucky and that was the case with EVOL.

I surely did not expect anything like to this to happen twice within the same year, but lightning did strike again. In November of 2005, I was once again running my trusty stock screener. I found a stock called EVCI Career Colleges Holding Corp. (NASDAQ: EVCI) which appeared to have some solid numbers, but it was the company's press releases that really caught my attention. At the time, the company was being investigated by the New York State Department of Education. EVCI had a fifty two week high of over eleven bucks, but it was setting new fifty two week lows near one dollar and eighty cents at the time. With such a precipitous drop in share price, I felt that the time was right to grab a few shares of this stock. Within a week of taking my initial position in EVCI, the company released promising results from an internal investigation regarding the New York State Department of

Education probe and the stock made a big jump. The positive news sent the stock to highs of $3.42. (see figure 17) Having taken an initial position at $1.80, I pounced on the opportunity to lock in a 70% profit. Fortunately for me, luck had struck twice. The action with EVCI was more than I had expected for the entire year. The fact that it had achieved such lofty gains in less than one week was amazing and I was happy to get out with a nice profit.

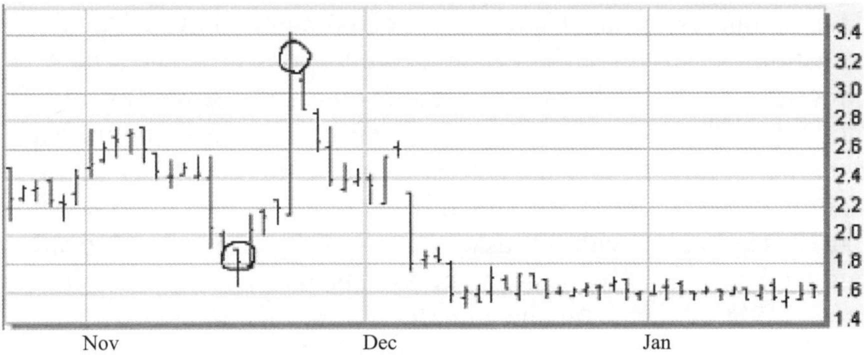

Figure 17: 3 month chart for EVCI. Initial entry point at lower left circle and exit point at upper right circle. Note the corresponding spike in volume on the date that EVCI achieved its biggest gains. On this particular date, as EVCI hit new highs I continually updated my stops to lock in a profit in the event that the stock fell. Such a strategy allowed for maximum profits.

Please realize that situations such as these are few and far between. I must say that for every EVCI and EVOL that I have ever owned, I have had just as many stocks tank immediately after purchasing them. I recall once buying a stock in a now defunct company called Net Gravity (NASDAQ: NETG). If I remember correctly, the stock was an online advertising company similar to Double Click. While I don't quite recall all of the specifics about this particular company, I do remember the stock tanking hard just a few days after I bought it. When the dust had settled, I believe that my wallet was about ten grand lighter!

So, now that I have explained why I don't put off purchasing a negatively trending stock, allow me to disclose my rationale for averaging down. In the vast majority of cases, the stocks that I purchase initially decline in value. As I am making the purchase during a sustained downward trend, this is not unexpected. I will often re-review the stock in question and if my confidence in the stock's fundamentals is reaffirmed, I will average down on the stock. The key to averaging down is to do it in small increments. A recent article critical of averaging down asked the question "When is the right time to average down?" The article presented a negatively trending stock and asked 'Do you average down here?" "How about here?" The article made the point that you don't know when a negatively trending stock will take a turn for the better, so there is no good way to time an averaging down purchase. I agree with this assessment and that is why I advocate averaging down in multiple small increments.

Let me give you an example of how averaging down once worked to my advantage. In January of 2004, I found a stock that I believed to have outstanding fundamentals. The stock was J2 Global Communications, Inc. (NASDAQ: JCOM) and, of course, it was in a downward trend at the time. Within a few days of purchasing the stock, JCOM took a sharp nose dive. While I did expect the stock to continue downtrending, I certainly did not anticipate such a quick decline. I reviewed JCOM's fundamentals and reread a few of its SEC filings. I felt confident in the stock so I added a few more shares to my holdings at the lower prices. As JCOM continued its slide I was beginning to second guess myself! Fortunately for me, the company soon held its quarterly conference call and my confidence in the stock was bolstered. Everything with JCOM looked great. It had outstanding P/E and PEG ratios, amazing growth, cash in the bank, and little debt. Despite these impressive fundamentals, JCOM stock continued to falter, due in large part to an increasing short position on the stock. Right then and there I made a conscious decision to average down in a major way. The strong fundamentals combined with the large short position led me to believe that JCOM was due to turnaround and make a nice run. I felt so strongly about this that I drove down to the local branch of my online broke and deposited additional funds into my account. As JCOM continued to fall I made multiple small purchases to average down my position. Over a one and a half month period my initial entry price of just over twenty seven dollars was averaged down to approximately twenty three dollars. In this process I also more than doubled my holdings of JCOM stock. With most of my investments I set tight stops, but I was not doing so with JCOM. Because I was averaging down my position, a tight stop would have defeated my purpose. In lieu of setting a tight stop, I closely monitored the stock. I would not recommend this tactic for those with weak constitutions as watching your averaged down position slowly decline is a harrowing experience. From my initial entry at twenty seven dollars, JCOM slid to a low of just under nineteen dollars. By averaging down, I had lowered my break even point and I had accumulated a large number of shares. On the downside, I had nearly doubled my investment in this stock and my risk was substantially increased. I took these actions with JCOM because I was confident in my due diligence. Of course, I could have been wrong and paid the price in the form of a huge loss. It would not be the first time and it certainly would not be the last. Fortunately, JCOM stemmed its slide around nineteen bucks and soon rose past my break even point. Once this happened I loosened my leash on the stock and monitored it less closely. JCOM had turned the corner and I knew that the shorters would soon scramble to cover their substantial short positions. This situation combined with renewed interest in the rising stock would allow JCOM to achieve a nice rise. Over the past two years JCOM has risen from its low of just under $19 to split adjusted highs eclipsing $60. (See figure 18)

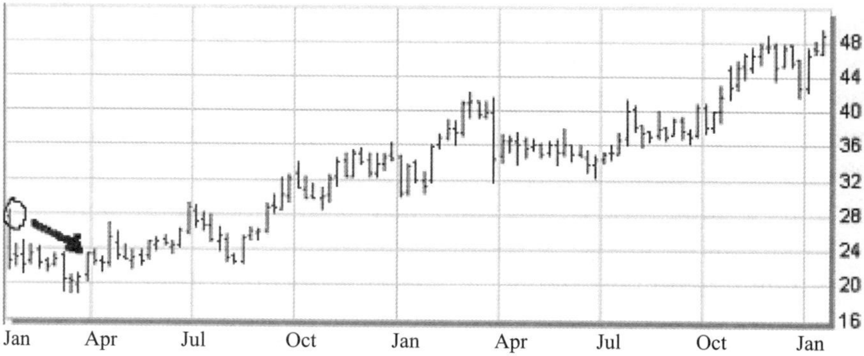

Figure 18: 1 year chart for JCOM showing initial entry point near 27 in January 2004 and subsequent averaging down over the next ninety day period. By averaging down, initial entry price of 27 was reduced to approximately 23. JCOM dipped to just below 19 prior to making a sustained positive run.

Averaging down worked well for me with JCOM, but utilization of this technique is not a foolproof endeavor. Believe me, there have been situations where averaging down has cost me quite a bit of money. Averaging down requires confidence in your investment. Review the company's SEC filings, listen to any available recorded conference calls, review recent press releases, and reassess your commitment to the stock. Occasionally, unexpected developments may change your outlook for a stock. If your stock posts disappointing earnings, for example, your initial assessment of the stock may be altered. This is a time to review your position. If you are still confident in your investment, averaging down is an opportunity to possibly increase your profits. The key to averaging down is multiple small purchases. If you make one large averaging down purchase you may limit your ability to acquire additional shares at lower prices should the stock continue to drop.

Some say averaging down is nothing more than throwing good money after bad money. In certain cases this may be true. If you have averaged down on a losing proposition, you must determine the point at which you will cut your losses and live to fight another day. Contrary to what some may say, it is my opinion that failure to consider the option of averaging down limits one's potential for additional profit.

10

PENNY STOCK SUCCESS STORIES

Undoubtedly, everyone that trades microcaps has a friend whose investment hit the bigtime. If fortune was smiling upon you, even you may have a few success stories to share. Microcap investing, particularly penny stock investing, has created immense wealth for many people. While there are plenty of folks that have lost it all, a number of investors have ridden their penny stock investments all the way to the bank. So what is it about certain microcap investments that allow them to break the mold? Why did these stocks rocket to riches while others lagged in the doldrums? Let's take a look at a few microcap companies whose stock prices have greatly appreciated and try to understand what set them apart from the rest of the pack.

Schick Technologies (NASDAQ: SCHK)

Schick Technologies (NASDAQ: SCHK) is a company that specializes in digital radiography (x-rays) for the dental profession. In layman's terms, SCHK makes equipment that allows x-rays to be taken and displayed on a computer. The development of digital radiography was a huge step forward for the medical and dental profession as the technology has multiple advantages over traditionally developed x-rays. With conventional radiography, patients are exposed to a significantly higher radiation dose than what they receive with digital x-rays. While a digital x-ray appears on a computer monitor instantly upon exposure, conventional x-rays require processing in multiple chemical baths for development.

In the field of dentistry, digital radiography has made great strides over the past decade. When the concept was first introduced to the industry, it was met with great resistance. To convert one's practice to a digital radiography set up, a dentist would have to purchase the computers, peripherals, and software needed to operate the system. Such a proposal posed a significant expense for initial installation. In addition to the initial start up costs, the industry had questions about the quality of the radiographs and there was concern that images could be altered with photo editing technology.

Digital radiography companies listened to the concerns of its customers and made adjustments. The quality of the images improved, the price of the software declined, and technology was implemented that prevented alteration. The concerns about the costs of computer hardware solved themselves as most dental offices installed intra-operatory computers for paperless record tracking and patient presentations. When they began to utilize the technology, dentists realized the advantages of digital radiography and soon embraced the concept. Digital x-rays eliminated the five minute waiting time for conventional image processing as digital images appear immediately upon exposure. This saved time, and as you know, time is money. Digital x-rays also eliminated the need for the many chemicals required to process radiographs. This not only eliminated the costs of purchasing the chemicals, it also eliminated the costs associated with their storage and disposal.

Dentists weren't the only ones who realized the advantages of digital x-rays. The dental insurance industry also caught onto the concept. The electronic transmission of digital x-ray images allowed for faster claims processing and improved communication between the companies and their clients. With the insurance industry advocating use of the technology, even the most reluctant dentists have been compelled to consider the application of digital radiography. As such, sales of digital radiography systems have significantly climbed in recent years.

One company that has successfully navigated the once choppy waters of digital radiography to the smooth seas of profit is Schick Technologies. Back in the year 2000, SCHK was a struggling company whose stock was relegated to the Pink Sheets. As is the case with many pink sheet stocks, questions about the company's future prospects were plentiful. Question one: would the dental industry ever embrace digital radiography technology? Question two: Would the dental insurance industry accept digital radiographs for claims processing? Question three: Could the company ever turn a profit and what about its debt issues? Question four: How can such a small company compete with established industry behemoths such as Kodak? Needless to say, this stock had its share of naysayers in its early days.

While questions about the future of the company were many, SCHK had the benefit of a strong business plan and persistent executive leadership. Rather than focusing on pumping the stock, as many pink sheet companies tend to do, SCHK focused on improving their product and growing the company. For example, in the year 2000 the company noted that they were experiencing a higher rate of returns for one of their top products. For some reason, the company's accuDEXA units were failing at an unusually high rate. Upon investigation of the potential causes for these failures, Schick determined that a combination of shipping damage and component sensitivity to humidity/temperature variations were the culprits. The company took measures to remedy the situation and the issues were soon resolved.

In all aspects of its business workings, Schick diligently searched for chinks in its armor and readily took corrective measures upon discovery of such matters. When it was realized that revenues had decreased substantially in fiscal year 2000, the company implemented several cost cutting measures including a reduction in its sales and research staff. The company also instituted tighter credit policies with non-dealer customers. Ultimately, these moves allowed Schick to reduce its bad debt from $5.6 million to $9 thousand. Compared to the actions that I have seen from many Pink Sheet companies over the years, Schick's moves were light years ahead of the pack. After getting their debt issues under control, Schick refocused its efforts on improving sales of its products. Expansion of sales through its domestic distributor and a significant improvement in international sales prompted Schick revenues to increase dramatically. As revenues improved, the company was able to expand its R&D efforts which led to the development of wireless digital sensors and fully integrated digital panoramic radiography devices. By 2005, Schick had quietly established reserves of $49 million and $60 million in working capital.

Schick's solid growth and its establishment as a leader in the digital radiography sector did not go unnoticed for long. In late 2005, Schick entered into a definitive agreement to merge with Sirona Dental Systems in a transaction valued at nearly $2 billion. As a combined company, Schick and Sirona would have 1,800 employees and revenues approaching $500 million. Not too shabby for a former Pink Sheet company! One interesting item of note is that in an older SEC filing, Schick specifically mentioned that consolidation of companies within the digital radiography and dental sectors was imminent. How right they were! The merger of

Schick with Sirona put the icing on the cake for this microcap success story. In just a few short years, Schick went from a fledgling Pink Sheet stock with a share price of a dollar to a full fledged member of the NASDAQ fraternity with a stock price exceeding $40. (see figure 19)

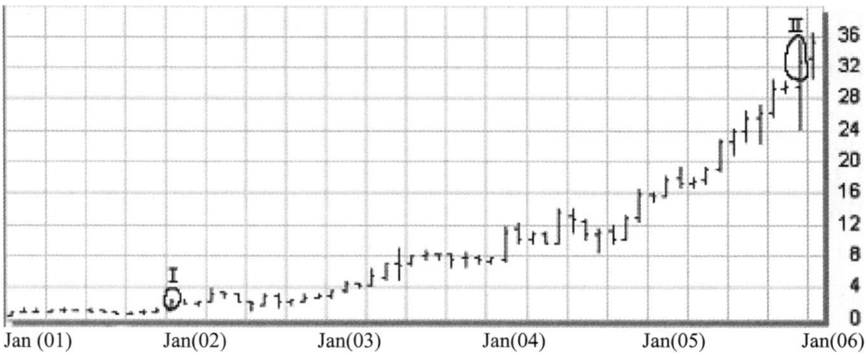

Figure 19: 5 year chart for Schick Technologies (NASDAQ: SCHK). Denotation I marks SCHK's transition from the Pink Sheets to the OTCBB. Denotation II marks SCHK's transition from the OTCBB to the NASDAQ. In June of 2006, Schick completed its merger with Sirona and its stock symbol changed to SIRO. SIRO recently traded at prices exceeding $40.

Birch Mountain Enterprises (AMEX: BMD)

A buddy of mine first told me about this stock when it was trading for eighty cents. He had originally bought it at twenty cents a few years before and he was sitting on a nice profit. I was impressed with his find and was surprised that he had not yet sold. After all, a 300% profit is nothing to sneeze at. My friend would hear none of it. He was not interested in selling. "Eighty cents is nothing" he said. "This stock is going to at least eight bucks."

I often find that when people have a good stock in their pocket, they always think that it is the best thing since sliced bread. With the old brand of penny stocks, holding onto a good thing for too long often was the road to ruin. I knew many investors that squandered immense profits because they knew in their hearts that their stock was headed "to the NASDAQ!" That was the battle cry back in those days. The NASDAQ was booming and everyone wanted their penny stock to make it to the show. In almost every case, penny stocks that had achieved big gains lost them in the bear market of 2000-2002. Stocks that were once trading at twenty bucks are now changing hands for just a few cents. Many of my friends lost all of their gains. I too fell victim to that terrible market. Many of my holdings were in small caps and technology stocks and the bear market gobbled up a good portion of my profits.

While the penny stocks of old were ripe for a quick rise and an equally quick fall, the penny stocks of today are somewhat different. Because of the stricter OTCBB listing requirements, the stocks that make up the OTCBB are now a stronger, more stable breed. When they rise, it is usually due to merit and not simple momentum as was the case in the old days. So my friend's stock had risen 300%. A few years ago I would have expected the stock to take a dive and fall victim to profit takers and shorts. In today's market, however, this was not meant to be.

The stock that my friend had told me about was called Birch Mountain. It was a Canadian company that owned a large parcel of land containing tar sands. My friend told me that this was "black gold", that the tar sands could be processed to make oil. At the time, I had never heard of the concept and it sounded a bit far fetched for me. I could not argue with success, however, as my friend had already made a nice profit with his investment. I performed a little due diligence on the company and the concept of converting tar sand to oil. I was impressed with what I found.

A portion of central Canada contains a rich resource known as "tar sand" or "oil sand". From this sand, it is possible to extract petroleum. With current output of nearly one million barrels per day, such deposits account for nearly half of Canada's crude oil production. Canadian estimates list a reserve of up to 175 billion barrels of oil within its sticky tar sands. Other estimates list up to 300 billion recoverable barrels and an additional 1 trillion barrels that may be recoverable with future extraction methods. Such an oil reserve would make Canada the largest oil rich country in the world. If you thought Canada was only good for exporting maple syrup, think again! Canada is poised to become an energy superpower.

While the technology to extract oil from tar sands has existed for some time now, it has rarely been used due to the fact that pumping liquid oil is a less expensive option. This is beginning to change, however. With the recent spike in crude oil prices to over $70 per barrel, extracting oil from tar sands has become a more attractive and feasible option. Improvements in mining and extraction technologies have significantly reduced production costs for converting tar sands to usable oil. In fact, Syncrude, a joint conglomerate of Canadian and U.S. energy companies, produced 77 million barrels of oil last year. "There's profit in them thar hills!" and companies are ready to take them. Birch Mountain is one of those companies.

Based in Calgary, Alberta Canada, Birch Mountain Resources (AMEX: BMD) holds the mineral rights to nearly one million acres of oil rich tar sand. In addition to the highly valuable tar sands, Birch Mountain also has over seventy years worth of limestone reserves and a mind boggling supply of aggregate, quicklime, and other various minerals.

As the Alberta tar sands region develops and expands its infrastructure, numerous construction projects including the creation of roads and bridges is anticipated. Construction of these roads and other infrastructure projects will require aggregate and Birch Mountain possesses some of the highest grade aggregate around. In the immediate vicinity of the Birch Mountain properties, the supply of aggregate is expected to fall 160 million tons short of demand. With enormous reserves of high grade aggregate, Birch Mountain is poised to eliminate this shortfall. In late 2005, Birch opened its Muskeg Valley Quarry for aggregate production and processing is expected to ramp up in 2006. While Birch Mountain has fresh untapped aggregate reserves, other quarries aren't as fortunate. In the vicinity of Birch's properties, there are two other aggregate quarries and both are estimated to have remaining aggregate supplies of less than ten years. When these quarries run dry, Birch will be the sole aggregate supplier for the region.

An additional product of the Birch Mountain properties is quicklime. Quicklime is used by tar sand processors for water treatment. Petroleum extraction from tar sands requires water that, over time, causes deposit formations on processing equipment. Quicklime is utilized to retard these deposits and current demand is estimated at 100,000 tons per year. Tar sand processors also utilize quicklime for desulphurization of gaseous byproducts. By the year 2020, the Canadian Energy Research Institute has estimated that up to 800,000 tons of quicklime per year will be required by the tar sand processors in the region adjacent to Birch

Mountain properties. Birch Mountain also possesses a unique advantage when it comes to quicklime as its nearest quicklime competitor is located over 550 miles from the tar sand region. The reduced transportation costs for Birch Mountain's quicklime will save its consumers $85 per ton. Not bad! Faster delivery and cheaper prices!

Birch Mountain stock has enjoyed appreciable gains over the past year. The company has done so well, in fact, that Jim Cramer, of TheStreet.Com and CNBC's *Mad Money* fame, has mentioned BMD. BMD is a true penny stock success story. While at one time trading for around a quarter, BMD has graduated from the OTCBB to the AMEX and has achieved a share price as high as $8.50. (see figure 20) With a market cap of over half a billion dollars, Birch Mountain has come a long way from its humble origins as an unknown OTCBB stock.

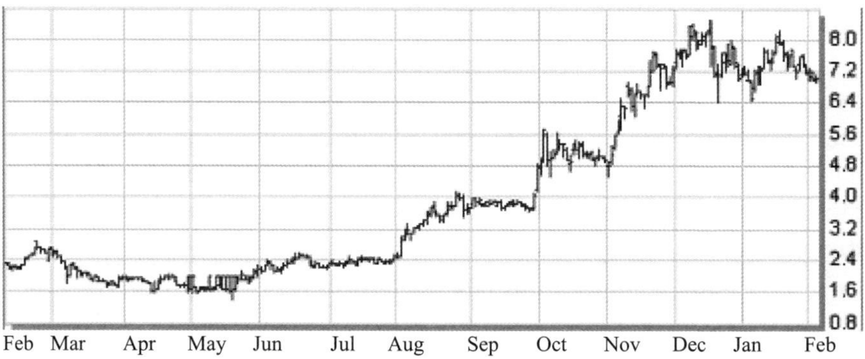

Figure 20: 1 year chart for Birch Mountain Resources (AMEX: BMD)

11

SECTORS POISED FOR FUTURE PROFIT

The dream of every investor is to identify the "next big thing" before it has become "the next big thing". Wouldn't it be great if you had picked up some shares of eBay or Amazon in 1995? Back then, who knew that these start-ups would become the business behemoths of the future? Questions about viability, debilitating debt, and public acceptance shied many investors away from these investments. However, there were a few speculators with a vision…a vision of e-commerce and the ability to market to the world via the internet. These investors did indeed identify the next big thing and now they are rich.

As history shows, stocks are much like fashion with fads that come and go. In the late 1990's anything and everything related to the internet was worth its weight in gold. After 9/11, anything related to security was the hottest ticket in town. Do you remember TASR? A few months after 9/11, this stock easily doubled and a few years and many splits later, this stock was a ten bagger! Wireless internet, nanotechnology…the list goes on and on. Some fads come and go while others establish themselves and become mainstream. So, the question is, what will be the next stock du jour and will it have staying power?

Of course, if it were easy to identify the hot stocks of the future, everyone would be rich. The truth is that identifying future trends is difficult, requiring research, insight, and a heavy helping of luck. I have identified five sectors that are poised, in my opinion, for explosive future growth. Within each of these sectors I have identified microcap stocks that may reap huge benefits if these sectors of the economy do take off as predicted.

DIABETES RELATED STOCKS

According the American Diabetes Association, approximately twenty one million people in the United States have diabetes. That is seven percent of our population! The number of people with pre-diabetes is nearly forty one million! When you add up the numbers, one out of every five persons in the U.S. either has diabetes or the precursor to the disease.

In 2002, it was estimated that diabetes had an economic impact of $130 billion. Although diagnosed diabetics only account for about 4% of the U.S. population, their healthcare costs comprised over 19% of personal health care expenditures. In 2002, direct health care costs for diabetics totaled $92 billion as compared to $44 billion in 1997. In just five short years, the direct costs for diabetic healthcare more than doubled. If only the stock market could provide such gains! Indirect economic costs associated with diabetes totaled over $40 billion, due in large part to the extensive number of lost work days caused by disease.

Classically, diabetes is associated with six different sequelae including micro and macro vascular disease (problems with the arteries and veins), nephropathy (kidney problems), neuropathy (nerve problems), retinopathy (eye problems), periodontal disease (gum problems), and poor wound healing.

These complications of diabetes can lead to a plethora of problems including blindness, cardiovascular disease, limb amputations, tooth loss, and sexual dysfunction. Did you know that diabetics are two to four times more likely than non-diabetics to die of heart disease? Did you know that diabetics are two to four times as likely to have a stroke and nearly three times as likely to die from that stroke? How about the fact that diabetes is the leading cause of blindness, end stage renal (kidney) disease, and extremity amputation? Diabetes is a nasty business!

Most of these problems arise when patients fail to adequately control their blood sugar (glucose) levels. Depending on the type of diabetes that afflicts the patient, blood glucose levels are controlled by different methods. For you see, diabetes can develop in one of many different ways. Type 1 diabetics produce no insulin and are dependent on the injected form of the drug to stay alive. Type 2 diabetics usually produce some insulin, but often in quantities that are insufficient to sustain normal body functions. Type 2 diabetics typically have a lack of insulin receptors, defective insulin receptors, or inadequate insulin production. These patients are usually treated with oral medications, diet modifications, and exercise. In many cases, injected insulin is not required in the treatment of Type 2 diabetics. When treating diabetes, physicians prescribe medication for the patient, but it is up to the patient to correctly administer this medication. Sadly, many patients fail to correctly adhere to the doctor's instructions, and hence, they often develop the problems that are typically associated with diabetes.

In the next fifty years, diabetes is expected to dramatically accelerate its prevalence in the US population. There are many factors associated with this expected increase. First off, let's discuss obesity. Obesity is strongly linked to the development of Type 2 diabetes. The National Health And Nutrition Examination Survey (NHANES) 1999-2002 found that 65% of Americans are "overweight" with a Body Mass Index (BMI) of 25.0 or greater. 31% of Americans have been identified as morbidly obese with a BMI of 30.0 or greater. Additionally, a concerning trend has recently been identified as nearly 16% of adolescents are considered overweight and an additional 15% are at risk of becoming overweight. This statistic has increased nearly 200% since 1980! The trend is clear…Americans are getting fatter. As our obesity rates increase, so too will the prevalence of diabetes.

An additional factor fueling the growth of diabetes in the United States is the rapid growth of the Hispanic segment of our population. Of those stricken with diabetes, Latino Americans are particularly at risk as they show a very high prevalence of the disease. According to the most recent U.S. census data, Hispanics are now the largest and fastest growing minority in the United States. Couple this fact with the finding that Mexican-American children and adolescents are more than twice as likely as non-Hispanic whites to be overweight and you have a recipe for increased diabetes development. As the Latino presence in the U.S. continues to grow, so too will the prevalence of diabetes.

The treatment of diabetes and its associated complications have become big business in the United States. Medical expenditures for diabetic patients are 2.4 times higher than those of non-diabetic patients. By the year 2010, healthcare costs related to the treatment of diabetes is estimated to grow to $156 billion. By 2020, this estimate nears $200 billion. The kicker is that those numbers don't even adjust for inflation!

With so much money being spent on this disease, it is not surprising that a large number of companies have entered the field of diabetes research and treatment. While many of these companies are NYSE and NASDAQ behemoths, most of the companies in the field of diabetes treatment and research are small microcaps. Some of these companies are biotech firms that are developing medications for the treatment of diabetes and its related sequelae. Some companies provide diabetic treatment supplies while others provide diabetic treatment services such as renal dialysis. Most of these companies are found on the OTCBB, but some are located on the pinks or the AMEX. One thing that each of these stocks has in common is huge potential. These stocks are microcaps in the truest sense of the word with market caps ranging from one to three hundred million dollars.

When all is considered, what we have here is a market sector that is ripe for the picking. I don't mean to sound crass by suggesting that we attempt to profit from a terrible disease, but the fact remains that this is a golden opportunity. We know from published data that diabetes is big business, comprising a substantial portion of nation's health care costs. The prevalence of diabetes is expected to increase dramatically over the next fifty years as obesity rates climb and the Hispanic population grows. What I have just shown you are things that big business have known for years. Why do you think that there are so many companies scrambling for a piece of the diabetes market? As most of the companies in this market are microcaps, I expect one of three things to happen. Scenario one is that the company will never successfully develop their therapeutic medications and they will go out of business. Scenario two is that the company will show promise and will be acquired by a much larger biotech firm. Scenario three is that the company will be successful in their endeavors, shun offers from larger firms, and move to a larger exchange in an effort to compete with these firms. Of the three envisioned scenarios, two offer great promise for investors.

Let's examine a microcap company that is poised to take advantage of the lucrative diabetes market:

Diabetes Microcap #1: Nutrition 21, Inc. (NASDAQ: NXXI)

When I originally discovered Nutrition 21, the company was dwelling in the doldrums and had recently received a delisting notification from the NASDAQ for failure to meet the $1.00 minimum share price requirement according to NASDAQ Marketplace Rule 4310c. As one would expect, the price of Nutrition 21 stock responded accordingly and a new 52 week low was soon established. Can anyone say, "Blood in the streets?" As I mentioned in my introduction to the diabetes section of this chapter, I am of the opinion that diabetic treatment stocks have enormous potential. As such, Nutrition 21 piqued my interest.

Nutrition 21 is a small biotech firm that derives most of its revenue from products that target the diabetic marketplace. The Nutrition 21 products Chromax and Diachrome are the company's flagship offerings. As their names imply, both Chromax and Diachrome are patented Chromium based formulations. According to the company, 12 published studies involving over 1,500 subjects have demonstrated that dietary supplementation with Chromax improves glycemic control. Similar results have been found with Diachrome. In fact, a June 2006 study found that Type 2 diabetic patients who took Diachrome had significantly better long term control of their blood sugar.

A unique aspect of Nutrition 21 is the fact that the company markets many of its products as nutritional supplements rather than pharmaceutical drugs. Such a tactic allows the company to utilize the Dietary Supplement Health and Education Act (DSHEA) regulatory pathway. Because the company classifies its products as dietary supplements, Nutrition 21 avoids the costly and time consuming process that the Food and Drug Administration (FDA) imposes on pharmaceutical medications. I, for one, find this to be a refreshing tactic. If you have ever owned a biotech stock, you are probably all too familiar with the endless waiting for drugs in the R&D pipeline to successfully navigate multiple phase clinical trials and the nightmarish possibility of a potential drug failing to show clinical benefits. Nutrition 21's utilization of the DSHEA regulatory pathway avoids these problems.

Over the past year, Nutrition 21 has enjoyed a tremendous recovery as retail stores such as Rite Aid, Albertsons, and Duane Reade have signed on to sell the company's products. Additionally, Wellmed, a physician-owned company that owns 10 clinics and provides management services to 18 additional clinics in the San Antonio, Texas area has signed a 5 year agreement to supply its Type 2 Diabetic patients with Nutrition 21 products. The fact that medical professionals who specialize in the treatment of Diabetes have chosen to include Nutrition 21 products in their treatment repertoire speaks volumes. They recognize the benefits of Nutrition 21 products. The best part is that these products are not drugs, they are supplements. No prescription is required! These products can be purchased over the counter like Flintstone vitamins. Most diabetics take enormous steps in an effort to control their blood sugar levels. As word spreads of the benefits of Nutrition 21 supplements, it is a pretty safe bet that many diabetics may utilize Nutrition 21 products.

About one month prior to the publication of this book, I noticed that others in the investment community were beginning to take note of NXXI. In June of 2006, an independent, non-compensated research report on Nutrition 21 placed a price target that was significantly higher than the stock's current position. Additionally, about two weeks prior to the publication of this book, Nutrition 21 was added to the prestigious Russel Microcap Index.

DENTAL STOCKS

One of my favorite sectors to trade is dental related stocks. This sector may sound pretty mundane compared to tech stocks, oil and gas stocks, etc, but this sector has been very good to me over the years. Unless you are a dentist, dentistry is a subject that no one likes to talk about. When you think of dentistry what do you think of? If you are like most people, you think of pain, needles, pain, root canals, and more pain. When I think of dentistry, I think of money! Over the past five years, some of my best finds have been in dental related stocks. I invested in Sybron Dental (NYSE: SYD) back in 2002 when the company was trading for as little as $12. Over the past few years, SYD has risen as high as $48. I found Centerpulse (NYSE CEP) at around 10 bucks back in 2002. Within a year it rose to around $30. The granddaddy of them all was Schick Technologies (NASDAQ: SCHK). I found SCHK when it was trading for under two dollars on the bulletin board. Since that time, SCHK graduated to the NASDAQ and recently rose as high as $45! Needless to say, dentistry and microcaps have proven to be a good mix!

As are most good investments, dentistry is a commodity that is also a necessity. According to the American Dental Association (ADA), dental expenditures topped $84 billion in the year 2005. Over the past ten years, dental health expenditures have more than doubled and are expected to approach $150 billion within the next ten years. With a nearly $70 billion influx expected over the next decade, there is great opportunity for dental companies. Likewise, there is great opportunity for investors to capitalize on dental stocks.

The dentistry of today is not your parent's dentistry. Long gone are the days of silver fillings and bulky plastic dentures. Today's dentistry has an aesthetic focus that is patient friendly. In the past, most people went to the dentist because they had to. A big cavity causing a painful toothache was often the impetus for a dental visit. The good news is that this type of situation is rapidly decreasing. With the advent of fluoridated water supplies, the prevalence of dental cavities and related dental maladies has significantly decreased over the past thirty years. Between 1971 and 1994, the prevalence of dental cavities decreased by 64%. From 1980 to 1995, the use of complete dentures decreased by 75% in 35-44 year olds and by 50% in patients over the age of 65. Hmmm. I know what you must be thinking right now. These statistics sound great when you consider the well being of the public, but how are they benefiting dentistry economically? If people have fewer cavities and are losing fewer teeth, how is the dental industry going to make more money? More importantly, how am I going to make a profitable investment in this industry if people have better oral health?

While it is true that the American public does have improved oral health, that does not necessarily mean that there will be less dental expenditures. With recent improvements in dental technology, dentistry has become a means by which one can improve both their physical appearance and their psychological well being. You have no doubt seen the television show *Extreme Makeover*. While most of the show's participants receive plastic surgeries ranging from nose jobs to breast augmentations, nearly all of the participants also receive dental work. Everyone wants a beautiful smile. To achieve such a smile, the dental industry now has multiple tools at its disposal. Digital x-rays, high speed tooth whitening systems, lasers, porcelain veneers, white plastic (composite) fillings, implants, painless computer controlled anesthesia, and invisible braces are just a few of the technological innovations attracting new patients to the dental profession. No longer are people visiting the dentist because they have to. Now people are visiting the dentist because they want to.

The aesthetic aspect of the dental profession is a great draw for many patients and is a huge reason for the recent increase in dental expenditures. As Americans continue to have improved disposable incomes, this trend is expected to continue. There is another trend developing in the dental profession that is only expected to get better in the near future. According to the U.S. Census Bureau, the "baby boomer" generation is now entering retirement age and is estimated at 76 million persons. Research shows that the baby boomers will have a longer life span and a substantially higher net worth than their predecessors. These statistics bode well for the Periodontics specialty of dentistry. Periodontics is a dental specialty that focuses on the treatment of the bones and gums within the mouth. With over one third of the U.S. population estimated to have periodontal disease, there is an ample supply of patients. According to the ADA, the utilization of periodontal services for patients aged 65 or older increased by 586% from 1980 to 1995. As the baby boomer population will soon swell the ranks of this age cohort, future utilization of periodontal services is expected to increase even more.

So what exactly is Periodontics? This specialty provides services such as "deep" dental cleanings (scaling and root planning), gum surgeries, and dental implants. Dental implants are small titanium posts placed within the bones of the mouth in order to replace missing teeth. The dental implant is a wondrous advancement in dental technology that has spawned numerous companies and generated billions of dollars for the dental profession. Dental implants involve more than simply sticking a metal post into a patient's jaw. When a patient loses a tooth, the bone that supports this tooth no longer has a function. As such, this bone will often "dissolve" away leaving the patient with a defect that is not suitable for a dental implant. In order to remedy this situation, the Periodontist may perform a variety of surgeries that repair the defect and provide the patient with a bony architecture more suitable for a dental implant. After an appropriate healing time, the Periodontist will place a dental implant that will later be restored with a porcelain crown. Voila! Where the patient once had an unsightly gap in his or her smile, they now have a beautiful tooth that often looks as good as, or better, than the real thing! Amazing, isn't it?

Another aspect of Periodontics that may draw a large number of future patients is the potential link between gum disease and other diseases of the body. Multiple studies have shown a positive association between periodontal disease and other diseases of the body including diabetes, cardiovascular disease, pre-term and low birth weight pregnancies, and preeclampsia. How is this so? How can bleeding gums affect the rest of the body? Periodontal disease is an infectious process that has the ability to seed the blood stream with bacteria and inflammatory mediators. As periodontal disease is chronic in nature, it has the potential to perform this deleterious process for an extended amount of time. Some studies have shown that periodontal treatment may reduce the risk of or improve the treatment of some of these diseases. If additional clinical studies confirm these initial findings, the medical community may begin referring a large number of patients to their local Periodontist for treatment. More referrals mean more dental treatment. More treatment means more money for the treatment provider. More treatment also means more utilization of supplies. More utilization of supplies means more orders for dental suppliers. Are you seeing the positive trend here?

One of the keys to making money with any investment is to anticipate future developments and seize opportunities before the general public realizes what is going on. With the affluent baby boomer generation now entering retirement and the advent of improved dental technology, it is a relatively safe bet that the dental industry is set to explode. Now that we have anticipated future developments on the horizon, let's take a look at a few dental related microcap stocks that are poised for big gains.

Dental Microcap #1: Bio-Lock International (OTCBB: BLLI)

Bio-Lok (OTCBB: BLLI) is a dental implant company which I feel has tremendous potential for appreciable future gains. To fully explain my excitement over Bio-Lok, I first need to tell you a little story.

As I mentioned earlier, I have had extremely good luck with dental related stocks. Back in the year 2003, I found a dental implant company named Centerpulse (NYSE: CEP) that was trending south. As you are well aware, I like stocks that are near their 52 week lows and Centerpulse seemed to be setting new lows on a daily basis. At the time, the company was mired in multiple lawsuits over alleged faulty surgical components and the stock was taking a big hit. I was aware of this company because I had personal experience with some of their surgical products. I knew that Centerpulse was a quality operation and was of the opinion that the lawsuits against the company would soon be resolved. In researching Centerpulse, I felt that the company had a strong bottom line and a good business plan. All things being considered, I was in a very fortunate position. I liked what I saw in Centerpulse and, thanks to the lawsuits, the stock was a bargain.

With its stock sitting at a price of around 10 bucks, I felt that one of two options was possible for Centerpulse. Option one was that Centerpulse would settle their lawsuits, return to business as usual, and the company's stock would rebound from its recently set lows. Option two was similar to option one in my assumption that the lawsuits would be settled, but in option two I envisioned Centerpulse being acquired by a larger dental implant company. At the time, the Centerpulse dental implants had some unique characteristics and I felt that a larger dental implant company would acquire Centerpulse for utilization of their patented technology. With the stock price depressed because of the lawsuits, I surmised that option two was the most likely scenario to unfold. The planets must have soon aligned because Centerpulse did settle their lawsuits and the company was acquired by a much larger dental implant manufacturer. When all was said and done, Centerpulse stock rose from around 10 dollars to a high of around 30 dollars!

So, what does this story have to do with Bio-Lok? Like Centerpulse in 2003, Bio-Lok is a dental implant company whose stock is extremely inexpensive. Also, like Centerpulse, Bio-Lok possesses patented technology unique to the industry. In 2003, I envisioned two options for Centerpulse and one of those options came true. In Bio-Lok, I am predicting a situation similar to that of Centerpulse in 2003.

Bio-Lok is a rapidly growing company that is gaining a foothold in the dental implant industry. Although revenues are relatively small at just over $8 million, the company's year over year quarterly revenue growth is explosive at +33.1% and the company recently reported record quarterly revenues in late June 2006. This revenue growth is attributed to Bio-Lok's recent expansion of its domestic marketing programs. As Bio-Lok has extensive relationships with many international distributors, past marketing efforts were traditionally focused on the international market. This philosophy changed, however, in the second quarter of fiscal year 2005 when Bio-Lok accelerated the implementation of its domestic marketing programs. The success of this dual marketing/sales effort in domestic and international markets is apparent as sales of Bio-Lok products increased by 46% in fiscal year 2005. As Bio-Lok intends to further expand its marketing and sales efforts in domestic, Asian, European, and South American markets, improvements in sales and revenue realization are expected to continue.

Bio-Lok dental implants are unique to the industry in the fact that they are designed and manufactured to allow for soft tissue integration. While all dental implants have the ability to integrate with bone, no other dental implants make the claim that they can integrate with soft tissue. The ability to integrate with soft tissue is highly desirable because it has the potential to improve the aesthetics of the gum tissue. As aesthetics have become the driving force behind the recent explosion in dental utilization, the ability to provide for better aesthetics makes Bio-Lok products a valuable commodity. With a current market capitalization of only $29 million, it is conceivable that a larger dental implant manufacturer could acquire Bio-Lok to obtain its patented soft tissue integration technology. In fact, a company acquiring Bio-Lok would obtain 27 actual patents and 8 patents pending. You think this sounds far fetched? I steadfastly disagree. Remember what happened to Centerpulse in 2003? Larger, more established companies often acquire smaller companies to obtain their patents and technological innovations. Such tactics provide the larger companies with enormous savings as they can reduce research and development time/expenses and get the newly acquired technology straight to market. Just as Centerpulse was acquired for its technology and patents, I feel that this could easily happen with Bio-Lok as well.

While speculative yet entirely plausible, the acquisition of Bio-Lok by a larger dental implant manufacturer is simply a prediction on my part. In making a more concrete analysis of Bio-Lok's short term future prospects, I like what I see. The current worldwide dental implant market is estimated at $1.4 billion and is expected to grow at an annual rate of 15-18% in the immediate future. With revenues of just over $8 million, Bio-Lok comprises a mere 0.5% of the current dental implant market. Talk about room for future growth! To achieve this growth, Bio-Lok has a multifaceted product integration strategy. To refer to Bio-

Lok simply as a dental implant company is somewhat of an understatement. While Bio-Lok does have a full line of dental implants and associated components, the company also offers a myriad of other dental products. To facilitate the placement of dental implants, Bio-Lok offers a wide array of precision surgical instruments and specialized variable torque handpieces and motors. To prepare sites in the mouth for future placement of dental implants, Bio-Lok offers products such as membranes and bone grafts to facilitate the reconstruction of bony defects. There you have it…complete product integration. From the initial step of intraoral implant site development to the actual placement of the titanium fixture, Bio-Lok offers the treatment provider everything necessary for successful dental implant therapy. With their recently expanded domestic/international sales force and marketing efforts, Bio-Lok will spread this message worldwide.

Bio-Lok offers the tools and components for dental implant therapy, but how do the implants stack up when compared to the competition? The top 5 companies in the dental implant industry make up 86% of the worldwide dental implant market. These companies are well established and have been around for dozens of years. Heck, one of these companies even has the original inventor of dental implant technology! With such stiff competition, can a small company such as Bio-Lok effectively compete? The answer is a resounding “YES!” A study released in December of 2005 directly compared Bio-Lok implants to those produced by 3i and Nobel Biocare. This study was a real life *David versus Goliath* scenario! Nobel Biocare and 3i are huge dental implant companies. In 2004, Nobel Biocare had revenues of over $400 million! Revenues for 3i are equally impressive. So how did Bio-Lok, a company with revenues of $8 million, compare to industry giants with combined revenues approaching three quarters of a billion dollars? According to the study published in the December 2005 issue of the peer reviewed scientific journal *Implant*

Dentistry, the Bio-Lok implants outperformed the Nobel Biocare implants and performed equally as well as the 3i implants. The study looked at engineering aspects of the dental implants such as functionally induced torque loss and compression/distortion of longitudinally sectioned joint architecture. The superior performance of the Bio-Lok dental implants proved the quality of their construction. An additional study proved the clinical performance of Bio-Lok implants. A 2004 study published in the peer reviewed scientific journal *The International Journal of Oral and Maxillofacial Implants* performed clinical and radiographic evaluations of multiple Bio-Lok implants over a 5 year period of use. In all aspects examined, Bio-Lok dental implants performed equally as well other implants in the dental industry.

With studies verifying the successful engineering design and clinical applications of Bio-Lok implants, what sets Bio-Lok apart from the competition? The answer is Bio-Lok's patented soft tissue integration technology. No other company has anything like it. This innovation will prove to be the key to Bio-Lok's future success. With the company's recent expansion of its sales and marketing efforts, the dental industry will become more aware of Bio-Lok's patented soft tissue integration technology as the focus of many dental practices continues to be that of an aesthetic nature. Without a doubt, I am confident that Bio-Lok's 0.5% penetration of the worldwide dental implant market is set to rapidly improve. I anticipate substantial appreciation for Bio-Lok stock and potential suitors for acquisition of the company as Bio-Lok gains market share in the dental implant industry.

When stock in Bio-Lok begins to move, what can we expect? In the world of microcaps, and especially for the realm of OTCBB stocks, Bio-Lok has an extremely small float (total shares available to the public for trading) with just over 8 million shares. Currently, Bio-Lock stock has a 50 day moving average of only $1.91 and a 3 month average trading volume average of around

12,000 shares. That's only $24,000 in trading activity per day! Despite this fact, Bio-Lock stock is up over 130% from its 52 week low. Just imagine what this stock would do with a little volume! Over the past 18 months, the most active daily trading volume for this stock was a mere 156,000 shares. With such a small float, even the modest trading volume of 156,000 shares caused this stock to spike upwards 25%. Imagine what would happen if 500,000 shares traded hands…or how about 1 million shares. Such volume would cause this stock would go through the roof! My bet is that volume in Bio-Lock stock will soon come. As sales continue to grow and the dental industry becomes more familiar with Bio-Lok products, profits should rise and I would expect the price of the stock to follow.

Dental Microcap #2: AFP Imaging Corp. (OTCBB: AFPC)

It's funny, over the years I have made many great trades by simply trading stocks that appeared to mimic other stocks. In the late 1990's I watched Yahoo make some significant moves, so I decided to look into search engine stocks. I ended up buying stock in both Lycos and Excite. Just like Yahoo, Lycos and Excite stock fared extremely well. The same thing happened with a stock called FONX. There was a time when voice recognition stocks were red hot. I remember seeing one particular voice recognition stock take off like a rocket only to be soon followed by a second voice recognition stock. I fired up my trusty stock screener and searched far and wide for stocks having anything to do with voice recognition. I found an undiscovered stock called FONX and it seemed to be the last voice recognition stock that had not made a run. I couldn't believe my luck with this find; it seemed too good to be true. At the time the stock had minimal volume, which did make me a bit leery, but I bought the stock nonetheless. I figured, why fight the trend? If voice recognition stocks were hot, this stock was going to be found soon enough. I picked up shares in FONX at a quarter. Within a few weeks, FONX was found by the investing public. I had beaten them to the punch! Just as the other voice recognition stocks had done, the FONX train left the station. When the dust settled, FONX had risen as high as $3. Not a bad little profit from making a simple observation.

A stock mimicking other stocks is not a new concept. It happens all of the time. In the late 1990's it was search engines, online brokerages, and e-commerce sites. After 9/11, anything related to homeland security made substantial gains. More recently, any stock that had a connection to the real estate boom was a safe bet for nice returns. One of the tricks to taking advantage of these situations is to recognize them before everyone else does. If you are buying a stock after you've heard about it on CNBC's *Squawk Box*, you are too late. While you are buying, the savvy investors who found the stock earlier are selling and thanking CNBC for the free advertising.

As you well know by now, I feel that the dental sector is a safe bet for considerable future gains. Many dental stocks have already achieved these gains, but there are a few dental stocks that have yet to be discovered. One of these stocks is AFP Imaging Corporation (OTCBB: AFPC). In the chapter titled *Penny Stock Success Stories* I chronicled the path that Schick Technologies (NASDAQ: SCHK) took from the Pink Sheets to the OTCBB to its final destination on the NASDAQ. Remember, this stock made a nice steady climb from $2 to $45! In AFP Imaging, I see striking similarities to SCHK.

Like Schick Technologies, AFP Imaging is a company that researches, develops, markets, and sells dental digital radiography systems. In comparing the two companies, I am reminded of what I saw in SCHK a few years ago…*before* SCHK made its huge run. In early 2002, SCHK was trading at around $2, very similar to where AFPC is trading now. At that time, SCHK had approximately 10 million shares of common stock outstanding. Currently, AFPC has about 12 million shares of common stock outstanding. In 2002 SCHK had revenue of $24.4 million and a net income of $3 million. Currently, AFPC has revenue of $23.1 million and net income of $1.9 million. While SCHK had total assets of $11.9 million and total liabilities of $9 million in 2002, AFPC currently has total assets of $8.1 million and total liabilities of $3.5 million. In 2002, SCHK revenue increased by 14.8% over the prior fiscal year. In their most recent SEC 10K filing, AFPC noted an increase in revenue of 16.6% over the prior fiscal year. In their SEC filings, both companies noted that reason for increased revenue was an increase in sales of their digital radiography products in both the domestic and international marketplaces. Comparing selling/general/administrative expenses, SCHK spent $9.5 million in 2002 while AFPC spent $7.1 million in 2005. Hopefully, by now, you get the point. In my opinion, the current status of AFPC is very similar to SCHK in 2002. To make things a bit easier, I have listed these similarities in a chart comparing 2002 SCHK to current AFPC. (figure 21)

In reviewing the chart, multiple similarities can be seen between the SCHK of 2002 and the AFPC of today. Going on the theory of stock mimicking, consideration of this chart should create excitement about the potential future gains for AFPC. From 2002 to 2003, SCHK nearly tripled in price from $1.06 to $3. From 2003 to 2004, SCHK rose from $3 to $7.45. From 2004 to 2005 SCHK improved from $7.45 to $16.50. In 2005, we know that SCHK agreed to merge with Sirona resulting in a $45 stock price. Disregarding that transaction, SCHK still rose to $24 on its own merit prior to the announcement of the merger. In just a few short years, SCHK rose from $1.06 to nearly $25. Considering that most investing experts consider a 7% yearly gain desirable, SCHK's return of over 2000% from 2002-mid 2005 is phenomenal. When you add in the additional gains from SCHK's merger with Sirona, a return of over 4000% was achieved! Will AFPC mimic the results of SCHK over the next few years? The answer, of course, is that no one knows. However, when you consider the similarities between the SCHK of 2002 and the AFPC of today, you should get a warm and fuzzy feeling inside.

	2002 SCHK	**2006 AFPC**
Outstanding Common Shares	10,144,520	12,345,994
Revenue	$24,399,000	$23,135,063
Net Income	$3,088,000	$1,899,930
Total Assets	$11,957,000	$8,153,396
Total Liabilities	$9,057,000	$3,490,765
% Revenue Increase	14.8%	16.6%
Selling-General-Administrative Expenses	$9,450,000	$7,155,537
Research Expenses	2,176,000	$435,813

Figure 21: Chart comparing the similarities of Schick Technologies in 2002 to AFP Imaging today. On a comparative basis, and after adjusting for a few years of inflation, the numbers for both stocks are very similar. Information for this chart was compiled from multiple SEC filings.

While I have noted that SCHK of 2002 and AFPC of today are eerily similar, there are some differences that I must also highlight. In addition to their dental imaging products, Schick Technologies also sells a Bone Mineral Density Assessment Sensor that helps to determine fracture risk for osteoporotic patients. Additionally, Schick sells a few products such as wireless sensors that AFP Imaging does not currently offer. On the same note, AFP offers products that Schick Technologies does not. In addition to their dental digital radiography line of products, AFP

Imaging also offers a full line of veterinary digital radiography products. According to the American Veterinary Medical Association, there are 73,000 Veterinarians in the US today. With a large majority of these Veterinarians operating a private practice, there is a huge opportunity for sales of veterinary digital radiography units. As a matter of fact, in their February 2006 SEC 10Q filing, AFPC noted a 7% increase in sales between the fiscal 2005 and 2006 six month periods, with a large majority of this increase attributable to its new general purpose veterinary digital x-ray systems.

Aside from comparing AFPC to SCHK, let's take a look at some exciting characteristics unique to AFP Imaging stock. AFPC has a total of 12.3 million shares outstanding. For an OTCBB stock, this total is microscopic! Of these shares, AFPC has a tradable float of less than 8 million shares. 8 million shares might not mean much to some of you out there, but to a seasoned penny stock investor, a float of 8 million shares is enough to make one salivate. A small float such as that of AFPC offers the potential for electric price movement. With any amount of substantial volume, AFPC could see tremendous movement in its stock price. As it currently stands, AFPC has a daily average trading volume of just under 20 thousand shares. That's a mere $40 thousand per day trading hands for this stock. In spite of this miniscule trading volume, AFPC stock is still up nearly 50% over its 52 week low. Just imagine what this stock could do with a little volume! Oh, one more thing, I know that I said I would quit comparing AFPC to SCHK, but I do want to mention one more thing. AFPC's current daily trading volume is very similar to that of SCHK in 2002.

OCEANIC SHIPPING STOCKS

A large number of oceanic shipping companies went public in 2005 when the oceanic transportation market was at peak levels. Since that time, shipping freight rates, and subsequently shipping stock prices, have declined appreciably. As their stock prices have declined, many of these companies have lost market capitalization value to a point that classifies them as microcap stocks.

As a sector, oceanic shipping stocks tend to fluctuate in value according to a combination of the supply and demand for shipped goods and the availability of vessel tonnage. When demand for the shipment of goods exceeds available vessel tonnage, freight rates increase, and as one would expect, shipping companies typically enjoy increased profits. An additional benefit of this situation is the appreciation in vessel valuation as many shipping companies supplement their bottom line through the sale of older vessels in their fleet.

A shortage of vessel tonnage typically lasts for a few years due to the fact that ship building is a slow process. Unlike the production of an automobile which can be accomplished in as little as a few months, ship construction and subsequent sea trials typically takes a few years. The increased demand and escalated vessel valuation seen during vessel tonnage shortages often lead to an overproduction of oceanic transports as shipbuilders attempt to cash in on the hot market. Upon completion of these ships, an excess of new vessels causes the supply of available vessel tonnage to acutely outpace the demand for the shipment of goods. As such, freight rates decrease as the market attempts to correct itself. Current research shows that worldwide demand for vessel tonnage typically increases at a rate of 4% per year. During times of increased shipbuilding, vessel tonnage may increase by as much as 10% per year. It does not take a genius to see that there is a discrepancy here. In an ideal world, demand for new vessel tonnage would equal actual new vessel tonnage production. Obviously, this does not happen.

It is evident that a cycle of feast or famine exists for shipping stocks. Cycles of high demand and vessel tonnage shortages seem to alternate with high demand and vessel tonnage excess. Reflecting these cycles, freight rates and shipping stock valuations fluctuate accordingly. From late 2003 to mid 2005, oceanic shipping enjoyed a situation of high demand and vessel tonnage shortages. As expected, freight rates increased and appreciation of shipping stock value soon followed. From early 2003 to late 2005 the index for dry bulk freight rates nearly tripled. In conjunction with this increase in freight rates, the valuation of some shipping stocks improved by as much as 2000%! These awesome gains could not last forever and they soon succumbed to the cyclical nature of the industry. Recent dry bulk freight rates have been more than halved from their highs of the 2003-2005 run. Likewise, although with a slight time delayed lag, shipping stock valuations have also declined.

Unfortunately, this downward cycle just happened to coincide with the initial public offerings of a number of oceanic shipping stocks. Companies such as Dryships (NASDAQ: DRYS) and Eagle Bulk Shipping (NASDAQ: EGLE) have seen their freshly minted shares painstakingly decline in value. In spite of the fact that most of these companies have outstanding P/E and PEG ratios, positive earnings growth, and increasing revenues, investors have dumped these stocks as they have taken note of the downward cycle affecting the industry. Some stocks have declined more than others and the time may be fast approaching to pick up shares in these companies. Many analysts would disagree with this notion as they are of the opinion that stocks must show a sustained upward trend before a buy signal is tripped. As you know by now, I like to buy stocks when there is blood in the streets and right now, the pungent smell of blood is beginning to permeate the air.

The downward trend for oceanic shipping stocks may continue in the short term and the upcoming year may present magnificent opportunities to buy shares prior to the next upward cycle.

Let's take a look at a shipping stock that is an excellent candidate for a strong rebound when the sector's cycle reverses.

Oceanic Micro Cap #1: TBSI International (NASDAQ: TBSI)

TBSI International (NASDAQ: TBSI) was one of the many oceanic shipping companies that had an initial public offering in the year of 2005. Joining TBSI in the oceanic shipping stock IPO frenzy were companies such as Quintana Maritime (NASDAQ: QMAR), Dryships (NASDAQ: DRYS), Eagle Bulk Shipping (NASDAQ: EGLE), and Genco Shipping and Trading (NASDAQ: GSTL). As I mentioned previously, 2005 was the beginning of the most recent downward cycle for dry bulk freight rates. As such, all of these recently IPO'ed shipping stocks have seen their share values significantly decrease. Please refer to figures 22 and 23 for a quick comparison of the recent performance of these shipping stocks.

Stock	IPO Price	52 Week Low	Recent Price
DRYS	~19.00	8.50	9.37
EGLE	~14.00	11.78	13.47
TBSI	~10.00	5.30	5.50
QMAR	~11.50	8.75	9.00
GSTL	~21.00	15.11	16.25

Figure 22: Oceanic Shipping stocks that had initial public offerings in the year 2005.

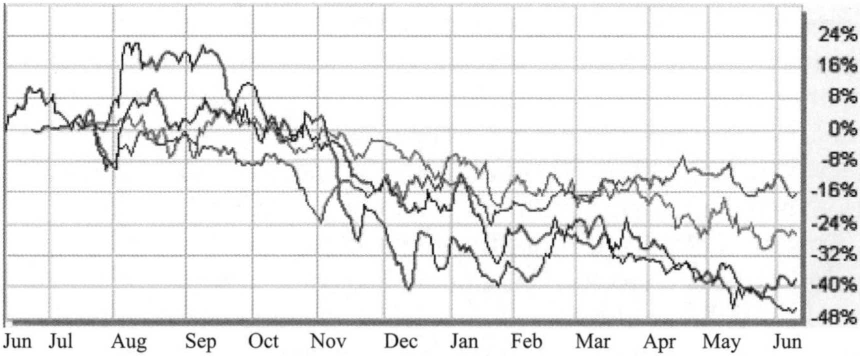

Figure 23: One year comparison of recently IPO'ed shipping stocks.
Genco Shipping and Trading Ltd. (NASDAQ: GSTL): ~16% negative return
Quintana Maritime Ltd. (NASDAQ: QMAR): ~25% negative return
Eagle Bulk Shipping (NASDAQ: EGLE): ~39% negative return
TBSI International (NASDAQ:TBSI): ~46% negative return

I found this sector when I ran one of my trusty stock screeners. I liked the numbers that I found with many of these stocks, so I delved a little further into the sector. My findings, which I provided in the previous section of this text, piqued my curiosity. Basically, all of these shipping stocks share certain similarities. If you were to invest in one of these stocks, which one would you choose? Let me tell you what I did to decide on which stock to pick. To begin with, all of these stocks were in a downward trend and, as you know by now, I like that when I considering an initial investment into a stock. Next, I tried to figure out which of these stocks was closest to the end of its downward trend. As I mentioned in the *Averaging Down* section of this book, trying to pick the bottom of a downward trending stock is very difficult. I looked at the IPO price for each of these stocks and calculated the percentage drop from this price. Of the stocks in question, TBSI and DRYS had dropped the furthest from their IPO pricing. As such, I focused my attention on these two stocks. I then compared the two stocks for their basic stock composition. I compared total outstanding shares, public float, and average volume. Next, I looked at revenues, cash reserves, and debt. Lastly, I read the SEC filings for both companies, researched their vessel fleets, and examined their principle cargo routes.

In comparing TBSI to DRYS I found many similarities. Both companies had similar share structures, cash reserves, and fleet size. DRYS had about five times the average daily trading volume of TBSI stock. This finding had some benefits for both stocks. As far as DRYS was concerned, a higher trading volume meant that the stock had better liquidity and told me that more people followed this stock. One would think that this would be advantageous for DRYS in my comparison, but I felt otherwise. The fact that TBSI had much less trading volume than DRYS led me to believe that many investors had yet to discover this stock. As most of their numbers were very similar, I saw no reason why DRYS should be trading five times as many shares as TBSI. With time, I felt that TBSI would achieve daily trading volume comparable to DRYS. With a fivefold increase in trading volume for TBSI, I anticipated a rise in its stock price. The final nail in the coffin for DRYS, as far as I was concerned in my comparison of the two companies, was the fact that DRYS had significantly more debt than TBSI. In fact, DRYS had approximately four times the outstanding debt of TBSI.

My find of TBSI occurred in late January 2006 at about $6.14. After performing a little due diligence, I told a few of my friends and colleagues about this stock. By this time, TBSI had dropped to $6. Even though the price of the stock was dropping, I was not worried. Like I said, I try to pick up stocks when they are trending south, hopefully at a price relatively close to their ultimate bottom. With my analysis of the oceanic shipping sector and my due diligence on the stocks that composed said sector, I felt that TBSI was a relatively safe bet for a sizable gain. I was not expecting a blockbuster here, but I was anticipating a relatively safe and respectable appreciation in price for TBSI. Over the next month, shares in TBSI stemmed their slide and reversed course for a 30% gain. Considering that most investing experts consider a 7% annual gain to be a desirable target, a 30% single month gain was outstanding! For many short term swing traders such a gain would be a respectable exit point. While a few of my friends and colleagues did make some trades with TBSI, I never did. A family emergency required my full attention and I missed the short lived TBSI run.

Although I missed out on some nice gains with TBSI, I did continue to periodically monitor the stock. In mid March of 2006, TBSI began to give back its recently acquired gains. Just after this happened, the broader markets began to slide. This combination of events proved most unfortunate for TBSI and the company's stock dropped nearly 34% from its high point in March of 2006. As I am typing this paragraph, TBSI stock is still in the midst of a tumultuous tumble. Have I purchased any shares in TBSI? Not yet. I am of the opinion that the combination of poorly performing markets and high oil prices will drive the price of TBSI down a bit further. I do believe that TBSI is setting up nicely for my particular taste in investing. The stock is trending south, it is setting new 52 week lows, and, in comparison to its peers (see figure 21), TBSI has taken the most dramatic fall. I know that those parameters sound crazy and that many investing professionals will question my sanity, but that is what "blood in the streets" investing is all about!

ALTERNATIVE ENERGY STOCKS

Alternative energy is a topic that has received substantial interest over the past few years. With the price of oil hitting new highs on a seemingly daily basis and the instability of many major oil producing nations, calls for alternative energy sources will surely increase in the near future. In President Bush's 2006 State of the Union Address, he stressed the need to promote energy efficiency, conservation, and the development of cleaner technology. Ultimately, this means that the United States must reduce its dependence on oil as a primary energy source. On many occasions during the year 2005, President Bush stressed the need of the nation to pare its reliance on foreign entities for oil. In one particular speech President Bush noted, "…sometimes we rely upon energy sources from countries that don't particularly like us." Additionally, he noted, "…we're running out of energy in America."

The American energy crisis prompted congress to pass an ambitious energy bill in July of 2005. Upon signing the bill into law in August of 2005, President Bush noted, "…we need to produce more energy. We need to diversify our energy supply, and we need to modernize our energy delivery." The new law gives $14.5 billion in tax cuts over the next ten years and provides incentives to various energy suppliers including those that supply alternative energy. Alternative energy sources are plentiful in number, but many are infantile in development or currently cost prohibitive. Energy production from solar and wind sources are well known, while other alternative energy sources are just beginning to receive attention. Clean coal technology, hydrogen fuel applications, and vegetable based fuels are just a few of the many alternative energy sources being investigated as a solution for our increased energy demands. Another alternative energy source receiving substantial attention is waste to energy production.

While we don't have as much oil as other nations, waste is one resource in which the United States is stocked in abundance. Recent reports estimate that the average American produces nearly1,600 pounds of trash per year. When you consider that the US population numbers nearly 300 million people, 1,600 pounds of trash per person really adds up! In addition to that, realize that this newly generated trash ends up in landfills that have immense reserves of waste from previous years of disposal. With such an enormous resource at our disposal, the application of converting waste to energy has been heavily researched and is just now beginning to reach fruition as a viable energy alternative. Although you might not know it, the US currently utilizes approximately 14% of its solid waste for energy production. Current US waste to energy production generates enough power to supply over 2 million households. So, if we have all of this garbage and we have the technology to convert it to energy, why isn't waste to energy more of a mainstream source of power? The answer is cost. As of now, it costs more to generate electricity at a waste to energy plant than it does to produce the same amount of energy from a coal, nuclear, or hydroelectric plant. This may soon change. With President Bush's call for increased utilization of alternative energy sources and the tax breaks/incentives appropriated by the 2005 energy bill, the cost of waste to energy production may soon achieve a competitive advantage over conventional electricity production methods.

While waste to energy production has received some attention in US markets, the technology has also been investigated by numerous foreign nations. For example, Great Britain's Department for Environment Food and Rural Affairs (DEFRA) recently released a 202 page report titled *Climate Change: The UK Programme 2006* citing the viability of utilizing waste for energy production. According to the report, "With increasing pressure to divert biodegradable waste from landfill, there will be opportunities to increase the recovery of energy from residual post-recycling waste." Additionally, the report notes that energy recovered from UK municipal waste accounts is expected to rise more than 300% by the year 2020. A January 2006 BBC News release quoted British Environment Minister Ben Bradshaw as saying, "…energy from waste should have a much clearer role to play in obtaining environmental value from some of our waste resources."

While Britain is just beginning to realize the potential benefits of waste to energy technology and the United States is currently utilizing it for a small percentage of its overall energy production, other nations have firmly embraced waste to energy technology. Japan leads the world in waste to energy utilization with 62% of its trash currently incinerated for electricity production. Not far behind, Switzerland uses approximately 60% of its solid waste for energy production. While not quite on par with Japan and Switzerland, France and Canada also use waste to energy production to supplement their energy needs.

Clearly, the application of converting waste to energy has worldwide appeal. Depending on their geophysical resources, the nations of the world have varied energy needs. While most countries do not have enough oil or coal to satisfy their energy needs, one resource that all nations have is solid waste. Utilization of waste for energy production not only satisfies the need for electricity production, it also reduces landfill waste accumulation and pares dependence on foreign nations for geophysical resources.

Let's take a look at one microcap company, a pink sheet company as a matter of fact, that is attempting to become the worldwide leader in waste to energy production.

Alternative Energy Stock #1: International Power Group (Pink Sheets: IPWG)

One company that is poised to reap the benefits of waste to energy technology is International Power Group (Pink Sheets: IPWG). Based in Celebration, Florida and with branch offices in London, England and Mexico City, Mexico, IPWG is a development stage company attempting to build waste to energy facilities on a worldwide scale. Such an endeavor is an enormous undertaking and IPWG has methodically laid the groundwork for its future success.

In June of 2006, IPWG contracted to purchase the waste to energy technologies of Anovo AB, Add Power, and Scrub Power. According to company reports, the Anovo technology is a turnkey waste to energy process capable of disposing of thousands of tons of garbage annually while producing multiple megawatts of power. An additional benefit derived from the functioning of this technology is the daily generation of thousands of gallons of agricultural and potable grade water. Think about those numbers…one IPWG plant utilizing Anovo technology will have the potential to eliminate the waste of tens of thousands US citizens while simultaneously producing much needed electricity and water. The best part, in addition to this being an environmentally friendly process, is the fact that IPWG stands to make money on nearly every aspect of the functioning of each plant. When IPWG takes in waste for processing, they collect a fee from the entities disposing of the waste. That in itself is an amazing feat. IPWG does not have to pay for the raw materials they utilize for the creation of energy…they actually get paid to take in the raw materials! As this waste is processed, IPWG can sell the energy and water that they generate. By 2008, the company is projecting the completion of one location with twelve plants. Net income from these operations is estimated to be hundreds of millions of dollars! By 2010, the company projects several locations with eighty four plants pulling in an estimated net income exceeding one billion dollars! Yes, yes, I know that anyone can make projections, but it is delivering on those projections that counts. Can a Pink Sheet company such as IPWG deliver the goods? Many prominent people seem to think so.

Over the past year, a number of highly respected people have joined the IPWG team. Many of these individuals left their positions at billion dollar corporations to become a part of this up and coming organization. For example, when IPWG acquired the Anovo AB, Add Power, and Scrub Power technologies, the inventor of this technology, Mr. Lennart Strand, joined IPWG as well. Mr. Strand held the positions of Chairman of the Board and Chief Technical Officer of another company prior to joining IPWG. Do you honestly think that this man would give up such lofty positions to join a company that wasn't going to deliver the goods? The same can be said of Mr. Christopher Duncan, IPWG's new Chief Operating Officer. Mr. Duncan left his position as a Managing Director at Marsh USA Inc. to join IPWG. Marsh USA is a $15 billion dollar member of the S&P 500! Again, it is highly unlikely that a person of such stature would forfeit his position at one of the top companies in the country to join another firm if he wasn't absolutely confident in its prospects.

One person of particular interest that was recently appointed to the IPWG board of directors is Sheikh Hani Ahmad Zaki Yamani. Shiekh Hani Yamani is the elder son of H.E. Sheikh Ahmed Zaki Yamani, former Minister of Petroleum and Mineral Resources of the Kingdom of Saudi Arabia. When you combine the appointment of a very powerful man such as Sheikh Hani Yamani to the IPWG board of directors with the recent news that IPWG has finalized all of the necessary procedures to establish a Saudi Arabian subsidiary named "IPWG Saudi Limited" and that this subsidiary has received approval from Saudi Arabian authorities to commence construction of waste-to-energy plants within the Kingdom, one must ponder the possibilities. According to IPWG, the Kingdom of Saudi Arabia needs approximately ten plants "strategically located" throughout the Kingdom. One aspect of the IPWG waste to energy plants that is especially beneficial to Saudi Arabia is the creation of water for agricultural purposes. A 2003 assessment of Saudi Arabian water needs found that approximately 70% of the Kingdom's water is supplied by coastal desalination plants. When pumped to inland cities, it is estimated that up to 50% of the pumped water is lost due to problems with the pipeline network. To meet the Kingdom's water needs over the next twenty years, it is projected that Saudi Arabia will need up to fifteen additional water desalination plants at a cost of over $900 million each. Could IPWG's press release concerning the "strategic location" of waste to energy plants be a hint that the Kingdom of Saudi Arabia is interested in utilizing IPWG plants as a means to deliver water to areas not accessible to water desalination plants? The appointment of Sheikh Hani Yamani and the creation of a Saudi Arabian subsidiary lead me to believe so. Think about what this could mean…ten plants in Saudi Arabia translates into a possible $3 billion in annual revenue! While this sounds great, don't forget that IPWG is targeting other countries as well. In late March of 2006, IPWG received initial approval to construct two waste to energy facilities in the municipality of Ensenada, Mexico. Hmmm. Could England be next? In January of 2006 IPWG opened a new office in London, England. With the recently released 2006 DEFRA report calling for increased utilization of renewable energy sources, IPWG waste to energy plants could be popping up in the English countryside!

With projected revenues in the billions and a horde of high profile individuals joining the company, I am sure that you are wondering why IPWG is a pink sheet company. The simple fact is that IPWG is a development stage company. It says so in the company's most recent 10K filing. As it is in development stage, the company has yet to prove itself. However, as mentioned before, IPWG is laying the groundwork for its future success. Acquisition of patented waste to energy technology, the appointment of powerful figures to its board of directors, an application for listing on the OTCBB…this company is taking all of the right steps in a logical and sensible fashion. If you are wondering why IPWG does not apply straight to a large exchange such as the NASDAQ or NYSE, go back to chapter four and read about the listing requirements for these exchanges.

I had the privilege of speaking with IPWG CEO Peter Toscano in June of 2006. With corporate offices in Florida, England, and Mexico, Mr. Toscano is frequently on the move so I felt very fortunate to speak with him.

Question: Mr. Toscano, you have recently been involved with companies that were quoted by the OTCBB and the Pink Sheets respectively. What advantages and disadvantages do you see between the two quotation services?

Mr. Toscano: First of all, being quoted on the OTCBB instantly provides a measure of respect to your company. This is especially important when you are trying to raise funds for your company. Many venture capitalists won't talk to you when they hear that your company is quoted on the Pinks. I once had a guy tell me to come back once my company had "grown up".

Getting a listing on the OTCBB is not an easy process. I had a company once wait for two years to get its listing on the bulletin board. In fact, I am currently waiting for IPWG to get the go ahead for its move to the bulletin board. We filed paperwork with the SEC in July 2005 and we are still waiting for approval! Those guys scrutinize you with a fine tooth comb before approving your listing.

Question: Are there advantages to being listed on the Pink Sheets?

Mr. Toscano: The good thing about the Pink Sheets is that it is easier to get an initial listing. You have the ability to get your stock up and running without the long wait of the bulletin board. Even though we are currently on the Pinks, we are a fully reporting company. Because of this, I think that we will have a smooth transition to the bulletin board.

Question: You have chosen to be a fully reporting company even though it is not required by the Pink Sheets. Why?

Mr. Toscano: I feel that it is very important for your company to be transparent. The stock is publicly traded. A company with publicly traded stock should make its information public. How can you ask someone to invest their hard earned money in your company if you hide information from them? That just doesn't seem right to me.

Question: So, are you saying that all publicly traded companies should be fully compliant with their filings?

Mr. Toscano: Yes, that is exactly what I am saying. If you have a publicly traded company, you must cater to the public. They should have full access to your filings so they can make an informed decision about your company.

Question: What is the biggest problem that you see facing OTCBB or Pink Sheet stocks?

Mr. Toscano: Without a doubt, it's the shorts.

CO-BRANDED MICROCAP STOCKS

A problem faced by most microcap companies is a lack of name recognition. With an unrecognizable name and/or product, companies have difficulty establishing their presence in the marketplace. Think about it, if you had to choose between two products, you would most likely buy the product with a name that you were familiar with. Research shows that consumers tend to make choices according to names and features that they either recognize or think that they recognize. Because of this, a strategy known as "co-branding" has been increasingly utilized by marketing experts.

Co-branding, also known as brand alliance, is a tactical measure employed by companies whereby they commingle their brand names in an effort to achieve improved marketability. Typically, the larger partner in the co-branding alliance will enter the relationship for strict financial gain as royalties or a percentage of sales are often paid to the company with the more recognizable brand name. While financial gain is also the ultimate goal of the lesser known company in the alliance, the benefits from the relationship go well beyond monetary matters. Recent research has shown that the mixing of brand names generates favorable perceptions for the co-branded product as the positive attributes of the well known product are transferred to the lesser known entity. These findings were corroborated by additional studies that found low recognition brands gain a substantially better evaluation when they are paired together with a highly recognizable brand.

The addition of a well known name brand to a relatively unknown product instantly makes the lesser known entity more attractive to the consumer. People tend to trust names that they know and they will buy products from companies that they are familiar with. Packaging emblazoned with the logo of a highly recognizable company or product assures consumers that the product is safe and of high quality. While consumers may initially purchase the product because of the highly recognizable co-branded entity, continued exposure of the product to the consumer allows them to become familiar with the lesser known company. Eventually, the consumer will associate the lesser known company as an equal to the larger more recognizable company.

Microcap companies certainly fit the bill of a weakly recognized entity. In getting their products to market, microcap companies face enormous challenges. Before a single sale is ever made, microcap companies must establish means by which to manufacture and package their product. This often involves expensive equipment purchases and the need for extensive financial backing. Once this is accomplished, the company must find an outlet in which to sell their product. This in itself can be a difficult process as large chain stores tend to purchase products that they are familiar with. A microcap company offering an unknown and unproven product is often a difficult sell for these large chain stores. If the microcap company can clear these initial hurdles, they then reach the really hard part...competing with the big boys. Right off the bat, microcaps are at a substantial disadvantage when their products are compared to those of well known corporations. Established products have the initial advantage of name recognition. From years of advertising, the consumer already knows about the established product. Most microcaps simply cannot compete with this. For starters, they don't have the sizable advertising budgets that large corporations utilize. Additionally, they don't have the history that established products possess. Without name recognition and an established history, the sale of a new product is a difficult task. A company may produce the best product in the world, but if no one knows about it, that product is not going to sell.

Over the years, I have been involved with a number of small startup companies that were trying to gain a foothold in the marketplace and all of these companies faced the challenges that I have just described. While all of these companies produced great products, the execution of the sale of these products was always a difficult task. One company that I worked with was trying to compete with the internet giant eBay. Talk about an impossible task! eBay has some of the best brand recognition in the business. Needless to say, this company was unsuccessful in its efforts. Another company that I once dealt with produced a line of paint and cement products that were in direct competition with well known corporations such as Quickrete and UGL. This company produced a line of high quality products that worked just as well if not better than the products made by the larger corporations. The small startup was tireless in its efforts and eventually landed a contract to have its products sold in a small number of Home Depot stores. Being the leader in home improvement product sales, Home Depot wanted to sell the company's products on a trial basis in a small number of its stores before committing to a nationwide order. While the company was initially bristling with excitement at the prospect of having its products sold in Home Depot stores, it soon discovered that having an unknown product sitting on a store shelf next to a well known and established product made sales difficult. A few of the product lines failed to sell and were eventually pulled from the shelves at Home Depot. Of the few products that did prove successful, the small company was unable to fill Home Depot's requests for additional inventory as a lack of working capital hampered the company's production, packaging, and shipping capabilities. Would this company have been more successful if it had co-branded with better known entity? Unfortunately, we will never know.

Some say that microcaps, especially OTCBB and Pink Sheet companies, don't have the capability to co-brand with large established corporations. These naysayers claim that most large companies don't want to be associated with a company that resides on the OTCBB or Pink Sheets. In many cases, this is an accurate assessment. However, there are always exceptions to the rule.

There have been a number of cases where a penny stock has successfully co-branded with a large corporation and turned that relationship into a successful endeavor. The first example that comes to my mind is that of Teleservices Internet Group (OTCBB: TSIG) in the year 2000. From what I recall, TSIG landed a deal with the Atlanta based Coca-Cola Bottling Company, a division of Coca-Cola Enterprises Inc, to perform promotional work for the Super Bowl. Talk about a co-branding bonanza...Coca-Cola and the Super Bowl together! Wow! You can't get much better co-branding than that and this relationship sent TSIG flying. Within about a one month timeframe, TSIG stock gained nearly 1900% in value! Unfortunately, this co-branding relationship was a short term endeavor and with the passing of the Super Bowl, TSIG and Coca Cola went their separate ways. Within six months of this insane run, TSIG had declined to the point where it had to perform a reverse split and change its stock symbol. While this example did not have a happy ending, it does effectively demonstrate the power of co-branding.

Without question, a microcap company that has enjoyed extreme success with co-branding is Bravo Foods International (OTCBB: BRVO). Bravo Foods International is an up and coming microcap that has fast become one of the most successful brand development entities on the OTCBB. Currently, Bravo Foods has co-branding alliances with industry giants including Marvel Comics, Masterfoods, and MD Enterprises. These alliances allow Bravo Foods to feature well known products and characters such as Snickers, Milky Way, 3 Musketeers, Starburst, Moon Pies, Spiderman, the Incredible Hulk, Wolverine, Daredevil, Electra, and Captain America on their products. I must say, that is an extensive and impressive list of powerful co-branding entities to have associated with one company's product line.

Bravo Foods effectively utilizes brand recognition to instantly compete with the big boys. In the realm of flavored milk products, Bravo is going head to head with industry giants including Nestle and Hershey. Face it, without the benefit of co-branding, Bravo would not stand a chance with such stiff competition. Over the years, Bravo Foods has experimented with a number of different co-branding partners. Six years ago, the company had products emblazoned with the lovable Looney Tunes characters. While the packaging featuring the likes of Bugs Bunny and Tweety Bird looked absolutely fantastic, Bravo eventually learned that such a co-branding strategy was not targeting the right audience. Through some hard earned lessons, Bravo discovered that while most adults enjoyed the Looney Tunes cartoons, they did not tend to purchase food products "endorsed" by their characters. Admittedly, the products were a hit with kids under the age of 5, but this age cohort just doesn't have much buying power.

When Bravo decided to change its co-branding marketing strategy, the company wanted to offer products that would set them apart from other flavored milk manufacturers such as Nestle and Hershey. Both companies offer a similar array of flavored milks ranging from their signature chocolates to vanilla, strawberry, and banana. Hershey also offers a chocolate "malted" flavored milk utilizing their Whopper brand of candy. Picking up on this marketing theme, Bravo decided to co-brand their flavored milk products with something that is both instantly recognizable and simultaneously irresistible to consumers of all ages...candy! Bravo teamed up with Masterfoods to offer milk products that are designed to actually taste like the candy featured on the label. To satisfy chocolate lovers and to compete head to head with the other chocolate manufacturers, Bravo introduced 3-Musketeers and Milky Way flavored milk products. To set them apart from the competition, Bravo then offered a number of flavors unique to the industry. With chocolate, vanilla, strawberry, and banana flavored milks being old hat, Bravo shook up the industry by offering a line of Starburst flavored milk products. As the only manufacturer to offer orange, mixed berry, and peach flavored milks, Bravo carved itself a unique niche in the industry. As one would expect, the candy flavored milks were an instant hit with consumers. Recognizing this, retail outlets have been lining up to sell Bravo's products. 7-11, A&P, Bi-Lo, Giant Food Stores, Piggly Wiggly, Safeway, Sam's Club, Shaw's, ShopRite, SuperTarget, and Walgreens are among the 30,000 retail outlets that now offer products made by Bravo Foods.

So far, I have only mentioned a handful of the products that Bravo Foods has to offer. While the cornerstone of Bravo's offerings is its Slammers line of candy flavored milks including Milky Way, 3-Musketeers, and Starburst flavored products, the company also offers Slammers that are flavored like chocolate or banana Moon-Pies. These are interesting flavors and should capture a segment of the market nostalgic for this regionally cherished confection.

To capture the market of active youths in the extreme sports mindset, Bravo Foods offers a line of PRO-Slammers products endorsed by well recognized BMX, inline skating, and skateboarding stars. PRO-Slammers come in chocolate, strawberry, and vanilla flavors and contain 50% more protein and 50% less fat than whole milk. With a combination of extreme sports marketing and intense nutritional value, the PRO-Slammers line of flavored milk products is ideal for sale in our public schools. Bravo Foods has made its intentions known that during the upcoming year, it plans to aggressively pursue this untapped market. Bravo Foods CEO Roy Warren recently said, "Slammers are a perfect fit for school a la carte lunch programs, providing superior nutrition and fortification with extended shelf-life, in attractive packaging that appeals to children and teens." Bravo's Vending and Schools division has been met with enthusiasm at schools around the country and we expect continued growth in the division as new markets are reached and products are better formulated for this marketplace." Think about it, as Americans have become increasingly aware of the obesity epidemic affecting our school aged children, a call has been made to offer healthier foods in our public schools. Many schools have proactively eliminated their nutritionally inept soda machines and replaced them with healthier alternatives. With a whopping 28 grams of protein, 50% less fat than whole milk, and fortification with 10 vitamins and minerals, PRO-Slammers are a perfect fit for our now health conscious public schools. Bravo's Slammers products are being vended through strategic partnerships with distribution and vending firms at approximately forty six schools in Florida alone. This is just the beginning. As there are over 108,000 K-12 schools in the USA, this market could prove to be a goldmine for Bravo Foods.

In order for Bravo to grow and expand, it must advertise. As an up and coming OTCBB company, Bravo does not currently have the budget for mainstream television advertising. To overcome this obstacle, Bravo has employed a grass roots marketing campaign utilizing alternative advertising strategies to reach potential customers. For starters, Bravo Foods is the official sponsor of a nationally recognized NHRA Pro Stock racer. With 23 races scheduled for the 2006 NHRA Pro Stock racing season, the Bravo Foods Slammers car will get plenty of "free" advertising from television coverage of the events. Continuing with the sports theme, Bravo Foods is also the official milk of US Club Soccer for the 2006 season. US Club Soccer, a National Affiliate of the United States Soccer Federation, registers competitive and recreational youth soccer players in 47 states and sanctions programs, leagues and tournaments throughout the year. With over 1,200 registered clubs and teams, US Club Soccer provides a great outlet for Bravo Foods to promote its flavored milk products to health conscious athletes and active youths. As an official product of US Club Soccer, Bravo Foods has joined an elite fraternity as companies such as Nike, American Airlines, and Budget Car Rentals also share this distinction. Last but not least, Bravo is also an official sponsor of the Washington Redskins of the National Football League!

An association with large, well established entities is the hallmark of a great OTCBB company. Masterfoods, Marvel Comics, US Club Soccer, The Washington Redskins…these are solid partners for Bravo Foods. Occasionally, the establishment of relationships with larger companies may lead to something more. An example of this is evident in Bravo's recently established association with Coca Cola Enterprises. In the fourth quarter of 2005, Coca Cola Enterprises began distribution of Bravo's line of Slammers products. Under the terms of the 10 year agreement between the two companies, Bravo Foods has granted Coca Cola Enterprises warrants to acquire 10% of BRVO's total authorized shares. Isn't that a nice thought? Coca Cola Enterprises, a $10 billion company that is the world's largest marketer, distributor, and producer of bottled/canned liquid nonalcoholic refreshments, has the potential to become a minority owner of Bravo Foods. If this occurs, one must also consider the possibility of Coca Cola Enterprises making a bid to completely acquire Bravo Foods. With annual revenues approaching $20 billion and an equally impressive market capitalization, Coca Cola Enterprises could easily acquire Bravo and incorporate their flavored milk products into their impressive array of beverage offerings.

When one considers all that Bravo Foods has to offer, the fact that this is currently a fifty cent stock is simply dumbfounding. Aggressive revenue growth, expansion into vast untapped marketplaces, associations with companies such as Masterfoods and Coca Cola Enterprises….what's not to like? This stock definitely has potential! Do me a favor. Make a trip to your local 7-eleven or Safeway and buy a Slammer. Drink the product, do some additional due diligence, and see if you agree with my assessment of this stock. I initially did this back when BRVO was trading for 14 cents. I remember thinking to myself, "I can buy 10 shares of BRVO stock for the cost of this one bottle of milk." In my opinion, it won't be long before the roles are reversed and it will take 10 bottles of Slammers to buy one share of BRVO!

Figure 24: Examples of Bravo Foods flavored milk products.

I recently had the pleasure of speaking with Bravo Foods International CEO Roy Warren. Here is an excerpt of my conversation with Mr. Warren:

Question: Mr. Warren, the last time I spoke to you, Bravo Foods International was called China Premium Foods. At that time, you were selling milk products that featured Looney Tunes characters. Do you still offer such products?

Mr. Warren: We changed our name from China Premium Foods to Bravo Foods International at the turn of the millennium. This change reflected a change in direction for our company. We discovered that by marketing our products with Looney Tunes characters, we were targeting the wrong demographic. We found that while characters such as Bugs Bunny and Tweety Bird were very popular with 2 and 3 year olds, they were not popular with older kids.

Question: Over the past year, Bravo Foods stock has enjoyed tremendous appreciation. To what do you attribute this amazing growth?

Mr. Warren: Our business has taken off this year. It is a culmination of our hard work starting to pay off. We have spent many years and invested millions of dollars into finding the right combination of product formulation, taste, target audience, and advertising strategy. Our co-branding alliance with Masterfoods and our distribution agreement with Coca-Cola Enterprises have also helped to fuel our growth.

Question: Who do you consider to be your major competitors?

Mr. Warren: We compete with Nestle and Hershey. Both offer flavored milk products in a variety of flavors. What sets us apart from our competitors is a difference in brand essence. While our competitors offer products with flavors limited to chocolate, vanilla, strawberry, and banana, Bravo has products that break the mold. Our co-branded Starburst, Snickers, Milky Way, and Moon-Pie flavors are unique to the industry.

Question: Bravo Foods is well known for its grass roots marketing campaigns. Can you tell me a little bit about these efforts?

Mr. Warren: The target demographic for most of our products is 15-25 year old individuals. We are trying to reach this audience through campaigns such as sponsorship of an NHRA Pro Stock Racing Team. We are also the official milk of US Club Soccer and a sponsor of the NFL's Washington Redskins. Our PRO-Slammers feature extreme sports stars and we sponsor a tour with BMX and skateboarding stars to promote these products to teens as a healthy alternative to sodas. Through these efforts, we hope to create a brand alliance that will last for a lifetime.

Question: There has been intense media focus on the obesity epidemic that is currently affecting our youth. Nutritionists have targeted public schools and are recommending that they modify their menus to offer more health conscious fare. Bravo products seem to be an excellent solution for this problem. Do you have any plans to tap into this burgeoning market?

Mr. Warren: Definitely. Our Vending and Schools Division has been diligently working with schools around the country. Bravo's products offer nutritional value that sodas simply cannot compete with. As schools begin to remove soda machines from their cafeterias, we would like to replace them with machines that vend our flavored milk products. Our products are already being sold in a number of Florida public schools and I feel that this is just the tip of the iceberg.

Question: Mr. Warren, where do you see Bravo a few years from now?

Mr. Warren: One of my goals is to market flavored milk as a beverage, similar to the way that sodas are marketed. Currently, milk products are treated as a food product. If you want something with milk in it, you have to go to the refrigerated section of your local grocery store. Bravo has the only shelf stable flavored milk product on the market, which means that our goods don't have to be refrigerated. I would like to see our products sitting on the shelves in the beverage aisle right next to the sodas. This would allow the consumer to purchase our product in bulk quantities. Of course, I would also like to see our product remain in the refrigerated section of stores for consumers that want a single serving beverage.

12

ONE FOR THE ROAD

I wanted to finish off this book with some information about a good old fashioned penny stock. While I do have the majority of my investments in NASDAQ and AMEX microcaps, I still like to look for great OTCBB penny stock prospects. Admittedly, these stocks are much harder to find than they were in the late 1990's, but there is no doubt that there are some potentially explosive penny stocks out there.

One penny stock that may be on the brink of a breakout is Reliant Home Warranty Corporation (OTCBB: RHWC). For those of you with a good memory, I did indeed mention this stock back in chapter 6. Currently trading at prices near a dime, RHWC is a true penny stock in every sense of the word. As most penny stocks do, RHWC trades on the OTCBB. So, why do I like this OTCBB penny stock? How do projected revenues approaching $1 billion and profitable operations grab you?

RHWC is a Toronto, Canada based corporation that originates, underwrites, funds, securitizes, and services sub-prime mortgages in select markets across Canada. Whoa there, I know what you must be thinking… "A *Canadian* mortgage stock? I heard that the housing market was going to take a dive! What is this guy talking about?" Just give me a few minutes and I think that you will like what you see.

First of all, what exactly is a sub-prime mortgage? A sub-prime mortgage is a type of loan targeted towards borrowers with less than perfect credit. In fact, for those with a credit score in the lower 600's or worse, a sub-prime loan is usually the only type of mortgage available. As the name implies, sub-prime mortgages are not top-of-the-line loans. Because their borrowers pose a higher risk due to their poor credit ratings, sub-prime mortgages have higher interest rates than equivalent prime loans and often contain specific provisions such as prepayment penalties and balloon payments. Sub-prime mortgages rose to prominence in the 1990's as lending institutions took advantage of changing regulations to extend credit to those with questionable credit histories. Depending on how you look at it, this could either be a good or a bad thing. On the good side, the sub-prime mortgage provides opportunities for home ownership to those who would typically be denied a standard prime mortgage and allows these credit challenged individuals the chance to reestablish a positive credit history. On the down side, a higher percentage of sub-prime mortgages fall into default or foreclosure when compared to standard prime mortgages. While this sounds bad, it must be noted that approximately 93% of sub-prime mortgages do not fall into default or foreclosure. Since their inception in the 1990's, the growth of sub-prime mortgages has been phenomenal with annual increases averaging 25%. In 2003, sub-prime mortgages comprised nearly 10% of all mortgage originations in the U.S. with a value estimated at $332 billion. While this dollar figure is higher than that in Canada, it does demonstrate the growing popularity of sub-prime mortgages.

So, if the borrowers of sub-prime mortgages pose an elevated risk, how is RHWC attempting to limit this potential pitfall? To assess the risk of prospective clients, RHWC utilizes specialized management software called Special Mortgage Application Reliable Technology (SMART). According to the company, the SMART application is a complete web based mortgage software system that enables Reliant to provide online mortgage brokers with easy-to-use auto adjudication origination coupled with a full in-house servicing, risk management and underwriting application software platform. Reliant CEO Boyd Sussanna noted, "Reliant's exclusive licensing of this front end web enabled software platform allows [Reliant] to cost effectively originate, service, underwrite and risk manage mortgages throughout the North American residential market. The SMART platform enables real time approvals and immediate service to our clients' needs." In other words, the Reliant SMART application limits the company's risk and allows much of its business to be conducted in a quick and efficient manner.

It's a good thing that Reliant has use of the SMART platform because the company may soon receive a flood of applications for its unique line of mortgage products. One such product is North America's first 50-Year amortization program for non-prime high-ratio mortgages. The decreasing affordability of the Canadian housing market may soon force consumers to take advantage of longer loans such as Reliant's 50 year amortization product. According to recent Canadian statistics, the housing affordability index has declined in most parts of the country including the provinces of Alberta, British Colombia, Ontario, and Quebec. Additionally, it does not appear that relief is in sight as it is anticipated that Canadian housing prices will increase by nearly 10% over the next 2 years. Despite the fact that affordable housing is declining in Canada, the Canadian real estate market remains strong. According to recently published reports, nearly 4,700 new homes and condominiums sold in the greater Toronto area in April 2006, a 2% increase over April 2005. Of these sales, a whopping 44% were attributable to high rise condominium/apartment sales. From first hand experience, I can tell you that downtown Toronto is booming. I recently took my family on vacation to Niagara Falls and Toronto. While in Toronto, we stayed in a hotel in the heart of the city and I must say that there were high rise condos going up all over the place. It was amazing! Over the years, I have lived in major cities such as Houston, Washington D.C., and Honolulu and I can honestly say that while I was in Toronto, I saw more new residential construction than I've ever seen in any of these other cities.

According to numerous Canadian housing reports, it appears that Toronto is not the only Canadian city experiencing tremendous growth. The Winnipeg housing market, for example, experienced double digit year-over-year price increases in the first quarter of 2006 while the Vancouver and Montreal housing markets also posted significant gains. One of the biggest Canadian housing booms may soon occur in the province of Alberta. Do you remember the story of Birch Mountain in chapter 10? The vast reserves of Alberta tar sand may soon fuel amazing economic growth in the province. As companies begin to mine and process the tar sands, they will need employees. These employees, in turn, will require homes in which to live. Shrewd speculators have already anticipated growth in Alberta evidenced by the explosive gains recently posted by housing markets in Edmonton and Calgary.

Recognizing that the Canadian housing market is experiencing nationwide growth, RHWC has teamed up with many of the top names in the Canadian mortgage and real estate industries. One such company is Centum Financial Group, Inc. Centum is one of Canada's largest mortgage brokerage institutions with over 100 locally franchised mortgage centers and over 800 mortgage professionals. According to the agreement, Centum will act as a Reliant Mortgage Lending Partner with a commitment to promote Reliant's mortgage suite products to its clients. With an anticipated $3 billion in mortgage originations over the next year, Centum has the potential to provide Reliant with a substantial revenue stream. Another Reliant partner is Stewart Title. Stewart Title facilitates title insurance and mortgage closing services for RHWC. With over 5,000 offices worldwide and annual revenues approaching $1 billion backing its Canadian operations, Stewart Title is a powerful partner for Reliant. Speaking of powerful partners, Reliant has also teamed up with international insurance giant Brit Insurance Holdings PLC. Based in the United Kingdom, Brit Insurance is a member of the FTSE 250 Index and has a market capitalization of $2.2 billion. Reliant's re-insurance treaty with Brit will provide default payment coverage for mortgages in the Canadian market originated and held under service by Reliant.

When you consider the fact that a small OTCBB company such as Reliant has the ability to land contracts with billion dollar corporations, you should be impressed. Another person impressed with Reliant is the company's official spokesman: Donovan Bailey. A 5 time world and Olympic track and field champion, Donovan Bailey was once deemed the fastest man on earth and is a national hero in Canada. Having Donovan Bailey as the spokesman for a Canadian corporation is the equivalent to a U.S. corporation having Michael Jordan as its spokesman. Mr. Bailey appears in Reliant television commercials that have aired on CNBC and regional television stations across Canada. For those of you who have a history of trading penny stocks, the last few sentences should have hit you like a ton of bricks. Over the years, how many OTCBB companies have you seen with a bonafide superstar spokesman? Additionally, how many OTCBB companies have you seen with television commercials? I can tell you that in all of my years of trading penny stocks, I have never seen a combination such as this!

The fact that RHWC is currently a 10 cent stock blows me away. Let me show you why. There is a NASDAQ listed company called Accredited Home Lenders (NASDAQ: LEND) that provides a glimpse of what Reliant has the potential to become. Like Reliant, Accredited Home Lenders is a company that originates, finances, securitizes, services, and sells nonprime mortgage loans. Although it is a relatively young company with its founding in 1990, Accredited has achieved revenues of nearly $600 million and a market capitalization of just over $1 billion. Not bad for a sixteen year old company! When you look at the key statistics for most mortgage related stocks, they tend to have market capitalizations that are approximately twice their annual revenue. This rough equation nearly applies to the numbers for Accredited Home Lenders. The same goes for New Century Financial Corporation (NYSE: NEW) and Countrywide Financial Corporation (NYSE: CFC). NEW has revenue of $1.3 billion and a market capitalization of $2.6 billion while CFC has revenue of $11 billion and a market capitalization of $23 billion. As you can see, in each of these cases, the market capitalization is approximately twice the company's revenue. I know that this is a very crude measurement, but let's apply this formula to Reliant. According to company statements, Reliant is projecting revenue of $750 million during its first full year of operations. With such revenue and our roughhewn revenue/market-cap formula, Reliant would have a market capitalization of $1.5 billion and a share price of nearly $9. From its current share price of a dime, a share price of $9 would provide a gain of nearly 9000%! Now, don't get me wrong. In no way am I suggesting that Reliant is going to have a future share price of $9. The previously mentioned mortgage companies are mature with well established market contacts and referral bases. At this point, Reliant is not as mature as those other companies. Reliant was founded in March 2005 as a stock exchange agreement allowed the current board of directors to assume control of the company. Over the past year, the company has worked diligently to establish contacts and referral bases that will set it up for successful operations similar to those of LEND, NEW, and CFC. In essence, Reliant has just recently opened for business. On July 21, 2006 Reliant launched its first residential mortgage product. This is a brand new company and we have the opportunity to get in on the ground floor! Even if Reliant only achieves half of its revenue goal of $750 million, the company would still provide investors with a handsome return according to the aforementioned revenue/market-cap formula.

To some, the thought of a penny stock providing quadruple digit gains may sound ludicrous. As crazy as it seems, the fact of the matter is that gains such as these do happen. During the internet boom of the late 1990's, this scenario played out dozens of times. Even today, some penny stocks are still making dreams come true. Over the past few years stocks such as SUF, SCHK, SDRG, IPWG, BMD, GRSR, and FTK have provided potential gains ranging from 2000-8000%! Will RHWC be the next penny stock that makes dreams come true? Who knows? What I do know is that the company looks pretty good to me!

Afterword

The world of microcap investing has changed dramatically over the past few years. While these stocks offer the opportunity for dramatic gains, their inherent volatility should limit their proportion in the composition of your portfolio. By no means do I advocate a nest egg composed entirely of microcaps. These stocks are not for everyone and those who are averse to risk would do well to stick with stocks that they feel comfortable trading. For those with the fortitude to take a little risk, however, microcaps offer the potential for enormous financial gain.

On a personal note, I would like to say that I hope you ignore the pompous crowd who feels that they are too good for microcap stocks. You and I both know that they are missing out on some huge potential profits.

Good Luck!

Dan Holtzclaw

Appendix A

Helpful Microcap Websites

When it comes to investing, there are thousands of websites out there. For the aspiring microcap investor, utilizing the right website can mean the difference between performing some legitimate due diligence and receiving a bogus tip on a dubious stock. So, which websites should you use? Which ones should you avoid? This appendix contains a description of websites that I find helpful for my microcap investments. I would like to mention that I have no affiliation with any of these websites and that I have not been compensated in any form for discussing them in this book. I am sure that I am leaving some great sites off of this list, but these are the websites that I currently tend to utilize:

1. **My online brokerage's website:**
   One of the best places to begin due diligence is on your broker's website. Each broker provides a cornucopia of research tools including stock screeners, interactive charts, access to SEC filings, data on insider sales, and more. You are paying for these services…you might as well use them!

2. **Yahoo Finance (http://finance.yahoo.com)**
I really like the Yahoo Finance website. It is simple, easy to navigate, and very user friendly. I have used the Yahoo stock screener to find many of my past investments. When I want quick and easy information about a stock, Yahoo Finance offers a number of options. Click on "profile" for a business summary, listing of the company executives, their age, and pay. This link also provides the address, phone number, and website for the company in addition to data on the company's index, sector, and industry membership. Click on "Key Statistics" for a review of the company's valuation measures, financial highlights, and trading information. Click on "headlines" for a review of the company's recent press releases. Click on "historical prices" for a detailed synopsis of the stock's pricing trends and trading volume patterns. Click on "SEC Filings" for access to the company's SEC filings. The list goes on and on. For a *free* website, the services offered by Yahoo Finance are outstanding!

Yahoo Finance also has over 6000 stock message boards. While Yahoo offers message boards for many microcap stocks, it does not provide message boards for OTCBB and Pink Sheet stocks.

3. **Motley Fool (www.fool.com)**
I like to read many of the articles offered on the Motley Fool website. As far as microcaps are concerned, the Motley Fool website discusses them quite a bit. This website offers many of the same features that other

financial websites provide, but I don't tend to use this one. You have to log into this site in order to access even the most basic of pages.

4. **The Street.com (www.thestreet.com)**
I liken this site to the Motley Fool website. I mainly access this site to read their articles. As always, Jim Cramer is very informative and entertaining. This website offers many of the same features that other financial websites provide, but I don't tend to use this one.

5. **Raging Bull (www.ragingbull.com)**
This is the granddaddy of all stock message board websites. There are thousands of message boards on Raging Bull. In general, this website has a message board for nearly every stock imaginable. If you find that Raging Bull does not have a message board for your favorite stock, simply submit a request for a new board and they are pretty good about getting one up. One thing that I like about Raging Bull is that it is frequented by tens of thousands of microcap investors, particularly OTCBB and Pink Sheet investors. This website is where a majority of the communication between microcap investors takes place. You can get a feel for the pulse of the penny stock market by perusing the boards on Raging Bull. One of my favorite boards on Raging Bull is *Niz's Billionaire Boyz Club*. This is a "hot tip" message board where traders post their recommendations and picks for the day. Literally speaking, this board receives thousands of posts per day. In its lifespan, Niz's board has received nearly a million posts! If you want to talk to some penny stock

investors, *Niz's Billionaire Boyz Club* is the place to do it! One thing that you must remember when visiting Raging Bull is that many of the posts on this website are baloney. Be very wary of what you read here. There are many unscrupulous characters that post here and they will take advantage of you if you are not careful. With time, you will learn how to separate the good posts from the bad.

6. Allstocks (www.allstocks.com)
I occasionally visit this website to view their message boards. Like Raging Bull, this website has a number of "hot tip" message boards that receive some heavy traffic. As a matter of fact, the *Micro Penny Stocks: Penny Stocks Under $0.10* message board recently had its 500,000th post!

7. Investors Hub (www.investorshub.com)
Investors Hub is very similar to Raging Bull. The site has many great message boards and usually has a different cast of characters than RB. A popular all-purpose OTCBB and Pink Sheet board on Investors Hub is *Hunchtrades*. *Hunchtrades* is a fairly active board with nearly 34,000 posts in the last year alone.

8. OTCBB (www.otcbb.com)
This is the official website of the OTCBB. The site contains OTCBB market news, statistics, company profile reports, and much more.

9. **Pink Sheets (www.pinksheets.com)**
This is the official website of the Pink Sheets. This site contains Pink Sheet market news, statistics, company profile reports, and much more. Additionally, this site also contains the link to OTCQX Pink Sheet stocks. One thing I like about the Pink Sheets website is the news link for quoted stocks. The Pink Sheets news link has all news that is related to a stock ranging from company generated press releases to SEC filings.

Appendix B

Microcap Stock Glossary

Ask: The price at which you can buy a stock.

Assets: Any possessions a company owns that have value.

Balance Sheet: A listing of all assets and liabilities for an individual or a business.

Balance Sheet Return: Sales/Price Ratio, Price/Book Ratio, Book/Share, Return on Equity, Profit Margin, and Reporting Date. These are all measures of company value and profitability.

Balance Sheet - Cash & Debt: Fiscal Year End, Quick Ratio, Debt/Equity Ratio, Current Ratio, and Cash/Share. Measures of the financial health of a company, particularly its assets and liabilities.

Basher: Someone who posts information in an effort to drive the price of a stock down.

Bid: The price at which you can sell your stock.

Block Trade: Usually, a trade of 10,000 shares or more. Penny stock block trades usually involve 100,000 shares or more.

Book/Share: The current fiscal year book value (or net equity for the corporation) per share of common stock.

Broker/Dealer: An agent who facilitates trades between a buyer and a seller and receives a commission for services. Dealers buy and sell for their own account and keep their own inventory of securities on which they can profit or incur losses. Most stock brokerage firms really act as brokers and dealers.

Buy-to-Cover: Purchasing stock to cover your short position. If you short a stock you must buy-to-cover in order to repay the brokerage the stock you borrowed from them.

Canceled Order: A buy or sell order that is canceled before it has been executed. A Limit Order can be can be canceled at any time as long as it has not been executed. A market order can only be canceled if the order is placed after the closing bell and is subsequently canceled before the opening bell of the following trading day.

Capital Stock: Amount of money or property contributed by stockholders to be used as the financial foundation for the corporation. It includes all classes of common and preferred stock.

Cash Flow: Net income plus depreciation and other non-cash charges.

Cash Market: A market in which security transactions occur within a few days of the trade date. Penny stocks trade in a cash market.

Class A/Class B Shares: Shares of stock issued by the same company but having some difference such as voting rights or a dividend preference.

Closing Price: Price of the stock at the close of trading for the day.

Commission: Fee charged by broker to execute your trade.

Common Shares: Represents the total number of common shares outstanding.

Common Stock: Stock representing partial ownership interest in a corporation. Ownership may also be shares with Preferred Stock, which has first claim on any dividends to be paid and, in the event of liquidation, to the distribution of the corporation's assets. Common stockholders assume the primary risk if business is poor, and realize greater gains in the event of success. They also elect the board of directors that controls the company.

Confirmation: A written notification from a broker to a client specifying the details of a stock transaction.

Current P/E Ratio: The ratio of current price divided by last two quarters earnings per share (EPS) plus next two estimated quarters EPS.

Current Year High & Low Prices: The highest and lowest price for a given stock during the current calendar year.

Current Ratio: A company's current assets divided by its current liabilities.

Date of Record: The date on which a shareholder must officially own shares in order to be entitled to a dividend. Most penny stocks do not pay out dividends however.

Day Order: The order will remain open for one trading day until it is executed or canceled. If the order is placed after market hours it will remain open for the next trading day. If it is placed during market hours it will remain open for the remainder of that trading day.

Deleted: A stock that is no longer included in The NASDAQ Stock Market.

Dividend: Distribution of earnings to shareholders, prorated by the class of security and paid in the form of money, stock, scrip, or, rarely, company products or property. The amount is decided by the Board of Directors and is usually paid quarterly. Most penny stocks do not pay out dividends.

Discount Broker: Brokerage firms that offer inexpensive transaction fees in lieu of not providing investment advice to clients. Most discount brokers offer online trading.

Dog: A stock that is not performing well.

Electronic Data Gathering, Analysis, and Retrieval EDGAR: An electronic system implemented by the SEC that is used by companies to transmit all documents required to be filed with the SEC in relation to corporate offerings and ongoing disclosure obligations. EDGAR became fully operational mid 1995.

Float: The number of shares a stock has available for trading purposes.

Gapper: The difference between the closing and opening prices for a stock on successive days. Stocks may gap up or down depending on the circumstances.

GTC: Good 'til canceled. A GTC order will remain open until it is executed or canceled, regardless of the number of trading days.

Held: A situation where a security is temporarily not available for trading and the Market Makers are not allowed to display quotes.

Hypester: Someone who posts information in an effort to boost the price of a stock.

Inside Market: The highest bid and the lowest offer prices among all competing Market Makers in a NASDAQ security, i.e., the best bid and offer prices.

Level 2 Trading: Type of service whereby an investor can view every market maker's bid/ask prices in real time and buy directly from the market maker of their choice.

Limit Order: An order in which you can set the maximum price you want to pay for your purchase, or a minimum price you will accept as seller.

Long: An investor who holds a stock for an extended period of time.

Limit Order: An order to buy or sell a stock at a customer-specified price.

Long Term Gain: A gain on the sale of a stock held six months or more and the profits are subject to the long term capital gains tax.

Market Order: This is an order that is executed immediately, at the best available price.

Market Makers: NASD member firms that represent a stock and compete with each other to buy and sell the stocks they represent. There numerous firms that act as OTCBB Market Makers. One of the major differences between the OTCBB and other major markets in the U.S. is the OTCBB's structure of competing Market Makers. Market Makers compete for customer orders by displaying different buy and sell quotes. Once an order is received, the Market Maker will immediately purchase for or sell from its own inventory.

Market Maker spread: The difference between the price at which a Market Maker is willing to buy a security and the price at which the firm is willing to sell it i.e., the difference between a Market Maker's bid and ask for a given security.

Market Order: An order to buy or sell a stated amount of a security at the current market rate.

Market Value: The market price; the price at which buyers and sellers trade similar items in an open marketplace. The current market price of a security as indicated by the latest trade recorded.

Material news: News released by a company that might be expected to affect the value of a company's stock or influence investors' decisions. Material news includes information regarding corporate events of an unusual nature, news of tender offers, unusually good or bad earnings reports, and a stock split or stock dividend.

MOMO Stock: Momentum mover. A risky investment strategy whereby a stock, usually unknown and thinly traded, is picked by investment clubs for intraday trading. Price fluctuations on these stocks can be very severe.

Most Active: Most active stocks usually by the number of shares traded per day.

National Association of Securities Dealers, Inc. NASD: The self regulatory organization of the securities industry responsible for the regulation of The NASDAQ Stock Market and the Over the Counter markets. The NASD operates under the authority granted it by the 1938 Maloney Act Amendment to the Securities Exchange Act of 1934.

Net Change: The difference between today's last trade and the previous day's last trade.

Net Worth: Surplus of assets over liabilities; what is owned free of debt.

Newbie: Someone who is a newcomer to stock investing; a novice stock trader.

Open order: An order to buy or sell a security that remains in effect until it is either canceled by the customer or executed.

Penny Stock: Name given to stocks that typically trade for less than $5. For the purposes of this book, penny stock refers to stocks traded on the OTCBB exchange for less than $1.

Pop: A quick gain in the price of a stock.

Previous Day's Close: The previous trading day's last reported trade.

Pump & Dump: Risky trading practice often seen with penny stocks where a security quickly rises in value based on unsubstantiated claims and then subsequently falls in profit taking sell-offs.

Real-time trade reporting: A requirement imposed on Market Makers to report each trade immediately after completion of the transaction. Stocks traded on The NASDAQ Stock Market are subject to real time trade reporting within 90 seconds of execution.

Resistance Point: The point at which a stock tends to stall in its rise to new highs.

Retained Earnings: Net profits kept to accumulate in a business after dividends are paid.

Securities and Exchange Commission SEC: The federal agency created by the Securities Exchange Act of 1934 to administer that act and the Securities Act of 1933. The statutes administered by the SEC are designed to promote full public disclosure and protect the investing public against fraudulent and manipulative practices in the securities markets. Generally, most issues of securities offered in interstate commerce or through the mails must be registered with the SEC.

Selling Short: Selling short is the selling of a security that the seller does not own, or any sale that is completed by the delivery of a security borrowed by the seller. Short sellers assume the risk that they will be able to buy the stock at a less expensive price than the price at which they sold short.

Spread: The difference between the bid and the asking prices for a stock. The spread is commonly influenced by the size of the float, demand for the stock, and current trading activity.

Stock Dividend: Payment of a corporate dividend in the form of stock rather than cash. The stock dividend may be additional shares in the company, or it may be shares in a subsidiary being spun off to shareholders. Stock dividends are often used to conserve cash needed to operate the business. Unlike a cash dividend, stock dividends are not taxed until sold. Most penny stocks do not have a stock dividend payment.

Stock symbol: A unique four or five letter symbol assigned to an OTCBB security. Definitions of fifth symbols can be found in Appendix C.

Stop: This is an order that converts to a market order once the stock trades at the stop price you have specified.

Stop Limit: This is an order that combines both the stop and limit order, in that once the stop price is activated your order can be executed up to your limit price. However, in a fast moving market, your trade may not be executed if the price goes past your limit.

Subpenny: Stocks that trade at one cent or lower on a daily basis.

Tanking: When a stock loses its value very quickly.

Ten-K Report (10K): Annual report that all companies must file with the Securities and Exchange Commission (SEC). This report contains vital company information such as financial statements, pending lawsuits against the company, company history, and future plans.

Today's High: The intra-day high trading price.

Today's Low: The intra-day low trading price.

Trading halt: The temporary suspension of trading in an OTCBB security. Only the SEC has authority to halt trading on an OTCBB security.

Volume: Total number of shares traded.

Yield: A return on an investor's capital investment.

Appendix C

Stock Symbol Additions

A - Class A

B - Class B

C - Issuer qualifications exceptions

D - New

E - Delinquent in required filings with the SEC

F - Foreign

G - First convertible bond

H - Second convertible bond, same company

I - Third convertible bond, same company

J - Voting

K - Nonvoting

L - Miscellaneous situations, such as depository receipts, stubs, additional warrants, and units

M - Fourth preferred, same company

N - Third preferred, same company

O - Second preferred, same company

P - First preferred, same company

Q - Bankruptcy Proceedings

R - Rights

S - Shares of beneficial interest

T - With warrants or with rights

U - Units

V - When issued and when distributed

W - Warrants

Y - ADR (American Depository Receipt)

Z - Miscellaneous situations such as depository receipts, stubs, additional warrants, and units.

Index

W

X

Y

Z